Using Prompt Engineering to Generate Ideas, Solve Challenges, and Innovate

Boost Creativity and Solve Problems Fast

Published by Angel Marqués
ISBN: 9798308402312

Hello! I would greatly appreciate it if you could share your opinion by leaving a review on Amazon. Reviews not only help other readers discover the book, but they're also essential for supporting future projects.

If you have a few minutes, please visit the review page by scanning the QR code below.

The Brainstorming Bottleneck

The Problem with Traditional Brainstorming

Traditional brainstorming methods have long been a cornerstone of workplace creativity. Teams gather in conference rooms, armed with whiteboards, sticky notes, and markers, hoping to conjure breakthrough ideas. The process seems simple: throw out as many ideas as possible, build on them, and filter for the best ones. However, the reality often falls short of expectations. Instead of innovation, many sessions yield recycled concepts, surface-level thinking, and frustration.

The limitations stem from fundamental flaws in the traditional approach. Groupthink is one of the most pervasive issues. In group settings, dominant voices tend to steer the conversation, often unintentionally shutting down dissenting ideas. Team members who might have unique perspectives hesitate to speak up, fearing judgment or rejection. As a result, the final ideas often reflect the loudest opinions rather than the most innovative solutions.

Time constraints further exacerbate the problem. Brainstorming sessions are typically confined to an hour or two, forcing teams to prioritize quantity over quality. Participants rush to contribute ideas, leading to a flood of suggestions that are often shallow or underdeveloped. The sheer volume of input can overwhelm teams, making it difficult to identify and refine genuinely valuable concepts.

Fatigue and cognitive biases also play a significant role. After just 30 minutes of intense brainstorming, most participants experience mental fatigue, diminishing their ability to think creatively. Cognitive biases, such as anchoring on the first idea or favoring familiar solutions, limit the diversity of thought in these sessions. These barriers undermine the very purpose of brainstorming: to generate innovative, out-of-the-box ideas.

In today's fast-paced, complex workplaces, these traditional methods are increasingly inadequate. As challenges grow more multifaceted, requiring input from diverse disciplines and perspectives, the shortcomings of traditional brainstorming become glaringly apparent. Teams are left grappling with outdated techniques that fail to meet the demands of modern problem-solving.

The High Stakes of Ineffective Brainstorming

The inefficiency of traditional brainstorming isn't just a minor inconvenience; it has real consequences for organizations. Missed opportunities for innovation can translate into lost revenue, stagnant growth, and an inability to stay competitive in dynamic markets. Companies that fail to innovate risk falling behind, especially in industries where rapid change is the norm.

For example, consider the tech sector, where new products and services are constantly emerging. A lack of fresh ideas can mean the difference between leading the market and becoming obsolete. The same applies to industries like marketing, healthcare, and education, where creativity drives value and impact. When brainstorming fails, entire projects can flounder, leaving teams scrambling to recover lost ground.

The impact extends beyond immediate business outcomes. Ineffective brainstorming can also harm workplace culture. Employees who repeatedly experience unproductive sessions may become disengaged, doubting their ability to contribute meaningfully. This disengagement can erode morale, collaboration, and trust within teams. Over time, the ripple effects can hinder overall organizational performance.

Why Traditional Methods Persist

Despite these drawbacks, traditional brainstorming remains entrenched in workplace culture. Part of the reason lies in its simplicity. The process is easy to organize and doesn't require specialized tools or expertise. Its informality also appeals to leaders who value participation over structure, mistakenly equating activity with productivity.

There's also a psychological element at play. Brainstorming sessions often feel productive, even when they aren't. Participants leave with lists of ideas and a sense of accomplishment, unaware that many of those ideas lack depth or feasibility. This illusion of productivity reinforces the cycle, perpetuating reliance on outdated methods.

Another factor is the social aspect. Brainstorming sessions are often seen as opportunities for team bonding and collaboration. Leaders value them as a way to build camaraderie, even if the creative outcomes fall short. However, this emphasis on social interaction can detract from the session's primary goal: generating impactful ideas.

The Call for a Better Solution

The modern workplace demands a new approach to brainstorming—one that addresses the limitations of traditional methods while embracing the possibilities of emerging technologies. As organizations become more complex, the challenges they face require innovative solutions that draw on diverse perspectives and expertise.

This is where AI enters the picture. Unlike traditional brainstorming, which relies solely on human input, AI-powered tools can augment creativity and problem-solving by providing data-driven insights, generating ideas at scale, and overcoming cognitive biases. By integrating AI into the brainstorming process, teams can break free from the bottlenecks of the past and unlock new levels of innovation.

The shift isn't just about adopting new tools; it's about rethinking the entire process. Teams must learn to collaborate with AI as a partner, using its capabilities to complement human creativity rather than replace it. This requires a cultural shift, where prompt engineering, iteration, and data-informed decision-making become integral to brainstorming.

The brainstorming bottleneck is a significant hurdle for modern organizations, but it's not insurmountable. By recognizing the limitations of traditional methods and embracing the potential of AI, teams can transform how they approach creativity and problem-solving. The next chapter will explore why AI is uniquely suited to revolutionize brainstorming, examining its ability to generate diverse ideas, analyze complex challenges, and empower teams to achieve their full potential.

Why AI Changes the Game

The Shift from Human-Only Creativity

Traditional brainstorming techniques are grounded in human creativity, collaboration, and intuition. While these elements remain valuable, they are inherently limited by biases, time constraints, and the boundaries of human cognition. Enter artificial intelligence—a technology capable of fundamentally transforming how ideas are generated, evaluated, and implemented. AI is not merely an enhancement to existing processes; it represents a paradigm shift in how we approach problem-solving and creativity in the workplace.

AI changes the game by augmenting human capabilities, providing access to vast datasets, and delivering insights that would otherwise remain hidden. It removes the bottlenecks that have long hindered innovation, such as cognitive biases, groupthink, and resource limitations. More importantly, AI democratizes creativity, making advanced tools and processes accessible to individuals and teams across industries, regardless of their size or resources.

The rise of AI-driven brainstorming marks a departure from the subjective and often chaotic nature of traditional ideation. Instead of relying solely on human input, teams can now collaborate with AI to refine their ideas, explore new perspectives, and make data-informed decisions. This chapter explores how AI reshapes creativity, enhances problem-solving, and paves the way for breakthroughs in the modern workplace.

The Unique Strengths of AI in Brainstorming

1. **Scalability of Ideas**:

   One of AI's most remarkable attributes is its ability to scale creativity. Unlike human teams, which can only process a finite number of ideas during a brainstorming session, AI can generate and evaluate hundreds— or even thousands—of possibilities in a fraction of the time.

   o For instance, an AI tool tasked with generating product ideas for a new tech gadget could produce concepts that span multiple domains, from design features to marketing strategies, all within minutes.

o   This scalability ensures that no potential avenue is left unexplored, providing teams with a wealth of options to consider.

2. **Data-Driven Creativity**:
    Traditional brainstorming relies heavily on intuition and past experiences, which can limit the scope of ideas. AI, on the other hand, draws on vast datasets, incorporating insights from diverse fields, markets, and cultures.

o   Example: A retail company seeking to revamp its customer experience can use AI to analyze trends, customer feedback, and competitor strategies, generating ideas rooted in real-world data.

o   By combining creativity with evidence-based insights, AI enables teams to develop ideas that are both innovative and grounded in reality.

3. **Breaking Through Cognitive Biases**:
    Human creativity is often constrained by cognitive biases, such as fixation on familiar solutions or over-reliance on initial ideas. AI disrupts these patterns by introducing perspectives that humans might overlook.

o   For example, AI can suggest unconventional solutions to problems, such as rethinking a supply chain model or exploring alternative markets, without being influenced by ingrained habits or assumptions.

o   This ability to think "outside the box" makes AI an invaluable partner in overcoming mental roadblocks and fostering true innovation.

AI as a Creative Partner

4. **Enhancing Collaboration**:
   Rather than replacing human creativity, AI serves as a collaborator, amplifying the strengths of individuals and teams. Through tools like natural language processing (NLP) and machine learning, AI can interpret human inputs, refine ideas, and provide feedback in real time.

   o For example, a marketing team could use AI to brainstorm ad campaigns by providing prompts such as "Generate three creative social media strategies to target Gen Z." The AI would then respond with detailed suggestions, which the team could further refine.

   o This iterative process fosters collaboration between humans and AI, blending machine precision with human intuition.

5. **Customizing Creativity**:
   AI can tailor its outputs to specific contexts, audiences, or goals. This level of customization is unparalleled in traditional brainstorming, where ideas often lack focus or alignment with strategic objectives.

   o For instance, a healthcare organization looking to improve patient engagement could use AI to generate ideas based on demographic data, patient feedback, and industry best practices.

   o By aligning creativity with context, AI ensures that the resulting ideas are not only innovative but also practical and actionable.

6. **Accelerating Ideation and Implementation**:
   In fast-paced industries, speed is critical. AI accelerates the brainstorming process by quickly generating and analyzing ideas, allowing teams to move from ideation to implementation more efficiently.

   o For example, a software development team working on a tight deadline could use AI to brainstorm user interface designs, select the most promising options, and even prototype solutions within hours.

   o This rapid iteration cycle shortens project timelines and enables organizations to respond to market demands with agility.

Real-World Applications of AI in Brainstorming

7. **Cross-Disciplinary Innovation:**
   AI excels at synthesizing knowledge from diverse fields, enabling teams to develop ideas that transcend traditional boundaries.

   o Example: In the automotive industry, AI could generate ideas for eco-friendly car designs by combining insights from engineering, environmental science, and consumer behavior.

   o This cross-disciplinary approach leads to breakthroughs that might not emerge from siloed thinking.

8. **Solving Complex Problems:**
   Some challenges are too intricate for traditional brainstorming methods to address effectively. AI's ability to process and analyze large datasets makes it an ideal tool for tackling complex problems.

   o For instance, an urban planning team could use AI to generate ideas for reducing traffic congestion by analyzing traffic patterns, public transit usage, and population density.

   o By providing data-driven insights, AI empowers teams to develop holistic solutions to multifaceted issues.

The Democratization of Creativity

9. **Leveling the Playing Field**:
   Historically, access to advanced brainstorming tools has been limited to well-funded organizations. AI democratizes creativity by making powerful ideation tools accessible to teams of all sizes.

   o For example, a small startup can now leverage AI tools to compete with larger corporations, generating ideas and strategies that rival those of well-funded competitors.

   o This democratization fosters innovation across industries, enabling organizations to unlock their creative potential regardless of their resources.

10. **Empowering Individuals**:
    AI also empowers individuals to contribute meaningfully to the brainstorming process, even if they lack expertise in a particular domain.

    • For instance, an employee with limited marketing experience could use AI to generate ideas for a campaign, providing a fresh perspective that enriches the team's overall creativity.

    • By lowering barriers to entry, AI enables diverse voices to participate in the ideation process, enhancing the quality and inclusivity of brainstorming sessions.

A New Era of Creativity

AI is not just a tool for brainstorming; it's a catalyst for a new era of creativity and problem-solving. By augmenting human capabilities, breaking through cognitive biases, and democratizing access to innovation, AI transforms the way teams approach challenges and generate ideas.

In the next chapter, we'll dive deeper into **"The Power of Prompt Engineering"**—the skill that unlocks AI's full potential as a creative collaborator. By mastering the art of crafting effective prompts, individuals and teams can harness the true power of AI to revolutionize their brainstorming processes and achieve unprecedented levels of innovation.

A New Skill for a New Era

Artificial Intelligence (AI) is revolutionizing the workplace, but its power lies in how effectively humans can interact with it. At the heart of this interaction is **prompt engineering**—the art and science of crafting clear, precise inputs that guide AI systems to deliver the most valuable outputs. Prompt engineering is not merely a technical skill; it is a creative and strategic discipline that determines the quality, relevance, and applicability of AI-generated ideas.

In this chapter, we explore why prompt engineering is the linchpin of effective AI brainstorming. We'll discuss its transformative impact on creativity, problem-solving, and productivity, along with the practical techniques that individuals and teams can use to master this essential skill. From crafting prompts that yield actionable insights to avoiding common pitfalls, this section delves into the nuances of communicating effectively with AI.

What is Prompt Engineering?

In essence, prompt engineering involves designing inputs—whether in the form of questions, commands, or scenarios—that direct AI systems to generate specific and relevant responses. The more thoughtfully crafted the prompt, the better the output. Unlike traditional human interactions, where context can be inferred, AI systems rely entirely on the clarity and specificity of prompts to understand what is being asked of them.

For example:

- A vague prompt like "Suggest ideas for a marketing campaign" might produce generic responses.

- A well-crafted prompt such as "Generate three innovative social media marketing strategies for a new eco-friendly clothing line targeting Gen Z consumers" provides context, audience, and focus, leading to more actionable results.

Prompt engineering bridges the gap between human creativity and AI capabilities. It allows users to frame problems in ways that leverage the

AI's strengths, such as processing vast datasets, identifying patterns, and synthesizing diverse perspectives.

The Transformative Impact of Prompt Engineering

1. **Guiding AI Towards Relevance**:
A poorly constructed prompt can lead to irrelevant, superficial, or unusable outputs. Prompt engineering ensures that the AI focuses on the right aspects of a problem, delivering results that are tailored to the user's needs.

o For instance, a product design team could use AI to brainstorm ideas by crafting prompts that include specific constraints, such as "Generate concepts for a portable coffee maker that weighs less than two pounds, uses biodegradable materials, and appeals to urban professionals."

o This level of precision ensures that the AI's output aligns with the team's goals, saving time and effort.

2. **Expanding Creative Boundaries**:
Effective prompts push AI to explore ideas that might not occur to human teams. By encouraging divergent thinking, prompt engineering unlocks the AI's potential to generate innovative solutions.

o Example: "List 10 ways to redesign a traditional classroom to enhance collaboration and engagement using technology and minimal physical changes."

o Such prompts encourage the AI to combine insights from architecture, pedagogy, and technology, producing ideas that transcend traditional brainstorming boundaries.

3. **Refining Outputs Through Iteration**:
Prompt engineering is an iterative process. Initial prompts often serve as starting points, with subsequent refinements improving the quality of the AI's responses.

o A team might begin with a broad question like "How can we improve customer retention in our subscription service?" and, based on the AI's initial suggestions, refine the prompt to focus on specific strategies, such as "Generate retention ideas that leverage gamification and community-building."

o   This iterative approach allows teams to extract increasingly valuable insights from the AI, making prompt engineering a dynamic and adaptive skill.

How Prompt Engineering Unlocks Creativity

4. **Overcoming Ambiguity**:
    One of the biggest challenges in traditional brainstorming is dealing with vague or incomplete ideas. AI, guided by clear prompts, can transform abstract concepts into concrete, actionable suggestions.

o   Example: A vague idea like "We should create a more personalized customer experience" can be refined into a prompt such as "Suggest three AI-driven personalization strategies for an e-commerce platform targeting millennial consumers."

o   The resulting output provides detailed, practical ideas that can be directly implemented.

5. **Encouraging Interdisciplinary Thinking**:
    AI excels at synthesizing knowledge from diverse fields, and prompt engineering can guide it to connect seemingly unrelated disciplines.

o   Example: "How can principles from video game design improve the user experience of an online fitness app?"

o   This type of prompt encourages the AI to draw on insights from psychology, user experience design, and gamification, leading to innovative solutions that might not emerge from traditional brainstorming.

6. **Enabling Rapid Prototyping of Ideas**:
    With effective prompts, AI can produce not just ideas but also initial drafts, designs, or frameworks.

o   For instance, a team working on a sustainability initiative could prompt AI to "Draft a one-page proposal for a corporate recycling program targeting employees across five office locations."

- The AI's output serves as a starting point, saving time and enabling the team to focus on refinement and implementation.

Practical Techniques for Mastering Prompt Engineering

7. **Be Specific and Contextual**:
   The more detailed the prompt, the better the output. Include relevant context, constraints, and desired outcomes.

   - Instead of: "Give me some marketing ideas."

   - Try: "Generate five unique marketing strategies for a startup offering eco-friendly home cleaning products, targeting young families with a moderate budget."

8. **Use Iterative Refinement**:
   Treat prompts as living drafts. Analyze the AI's responses, identify gaps, and revise the prompt to address them.

   - Initial Prompt: "What are some ways to improve employee productivity?"

   - Refined Prompt: "What are three cost-effective strategies to improve productivity among remote employees in the tech industry?"

9. **Experiment with Perspective Shifts**:
   Encourage the AI to approach problems from different angles by specifying roles or scenarios.

   - Example: "As a sustainability expert, suggest three strategies for reducing waste in a manufacturing process."

   - This technique adds depth and diversity to the AI's outputs.

10. **Balance Constraints and Creativity**:
    While constraints are essential for focus, overly restrictive prompts can stifle creativity. Strike a balance by providing enough structure to guide the AI without limiting its exploratory potential.

    - Example: "List innovative ideas for a smart home device that enhances convenience, security, and sustainability, with a price point under $500."

Prompt engineering is more than a technical skill—it's a creative partnership between humans and AI. By mastering the art of crafting precise, contextual, and iterative prompts, individuals and teams can unlock the full potential of AI for brainstorming and problem-solving. In the process, they transform the AI from a tool into a collaborator, capable of elevating workplace creativity to unprecedented heights.

In the next chapter, we'll explore "Implementing AI-Driven Brainstorming in the Workplace," diving into the practical steps, tools, and cultural shifts needed to integrate AI-powered ideation into everyday workflows.

Part 1: The Foundations of AI Brainstorming

Understanding AI as a Creative Partner

In an era where the demand for innovation often outpaces the human capacity to generate ideas, artificial intelligence (AI) emerges as a transformative ally. While AI's contributions to automation and data analysis are widely acknowledged, its potential as a creative partner remains underexplored. Yet, as organizations and individuals navigate increasingly complex challenges, AI offers unprecedented opportunities to rethink how creativity itself can be approached.

Creativity, in its essence, is about forming connections between seemingly unrelated concepts to produce something novel and valuable. For centuries, this has been the domain of human ingenuity, shaped by emotion, intuition, and unique lived experiences. However, the introduction of AI into the creative process challenges traditional paradigms. AI doesn't create as humans do—it doesn't dream, feel, or imagine—but it excels at rapidly analyzing patterns, synthesizing information, and proposing innovative possibilities that humans might overlook.

By positioning AI as a collaborator rather than a competitor, individuals and teams can unlock new realms of possibility. The key lies in understanding how AI "thinks," how it generates ideas, and how it complements rather than replaces human creativity. This partnership doesn't dilute human ingenuity; it magnifies it, enabling breakthroughs that neither humans nor machines could achieve alone.

Why AI in Creativity?

Traditional brainstorming methods, while effective in many contexts, often struggle under the weight of today's complexity. Teams gather in rooms, armed with whiteboards and post-it notes, hoping to spark brilliance through collaboration. While this approach has its merits, it's often constrained by group dynamics, cognitive biases, and time pressures. Enter AI, a tool capable of generating and refining ideas at scale, unhindered by the limitations of human memory or energy.

For example, consider a product development team tasked with designing an eco-friendly packaging solution. Traditional methods might involve a few sessions of brainstorming, with participants proposing ideas based on their knowledge and experience. While these sessions can be productive, they're often limited by the scope of the participants' expertise. An AI tool, on the other hand, can analyze millions of data points—from emerging materials science research to consumer preferences—and suggest innovative solutions that the team might never have considered.

A Partner, Not a Replacement

The notion that AI could replace human creativity is not only misguided but fundamentally misunderstands the nature of both AI and creativity. AI lacks the emotional depth, intuition, and cultural context that define human innovation. It doesn't experience "a-ha" moments or draw inspiration from personal memories. Instead, its strength lies in its ability to process and recombine vast amounts of information at speeds no human could match.

Think of AI as a powerful amplifier. It takes the raw inputs provided by humans—ideas, constraints, and goals—and generates outputs that push the boundaries of what might otherwise be possible. But these outputs are not final answers; they're starting points, sparks that require human judgment, refinement, and creativity to fully realize their potential. In this sense, AI doesn't diminish the role of the human creator; it enhances it.

By reframing AI as a partner rather than a replacement, individuals and teams can approach the technology with curiosity and confidence. Instead of fearing obsolescence, they can embrace the collaborative potential of human-AI interaction, leveraging the unique strengths of each to achieve extraordinary results.

The Evolution of AI in Creative Industries

AI's role in creativity is not hypothetical; it's already reshaping industries. In marketing, AI tools generate hundreds of ad copy variations in seconds, allowing teams to test and iterate at unprecedented speeds. In design, AI assists architects in creating sustainable structures by analyzing environmental data and proposing efficient configurations. In entertainment, AI algorithms help filmmakers craft more engaging narratives by predicting audience reactions to different plot points.

These examples illustrate a crucial point: AI doesn't operate in isolation. Its outputs are the result of human inputs, whether in the form of data, prompts, or feedback. The success of AI-assisted creativity depends on the quality of this collaboration. Just as a great musician brings out the best in their instrument, a skilled user can harness AI to unlock new dimensions of creative potential.

The Path Ahead

As AI continues to evolve, its role in the creative process will only deepen. But the journey is not without challenges. Ethical considerations, such as the risk of bias in AI-generated ideas, and practical concerns, like the need for human oversight, must be addressed. These issues, however, should not overshadow the immense possibilities that AI brings to the table.

By embracing AI as a creative partner, we can reimagine what's possible—not just in terms of what we create, but how we create. This partnership invites us to expand the boundaries of innovation, to approach problems with fresh perspectives, and to achieve outcomes that are richer, more nuanced, and more impactful than ever before.

The revolution is already underway. The question is not whether AI can be a creative partner, but how we can best harness its potential to shape the future of creativity.

How AI "Thinks" and Generates Ideas

To truly harness the creative power of artificial intelligence, it is essential to understand how it "thinks." While AI does not possess consciousness, emotions, or intuition like humans, it employs highly sophisticated processes to generate ideas and insights. By demystifying these processes, we can better appreciate AI's role in brainstorming and innovation.

The Fundamentals of AI Thinking

At its heart, AI "thinks" through algorithms and models designed to identify patterns, analyze data, and predict outcomes. Machine learning, a subset of AI, relies on training data to build models that can process and interpret new information. This process includes several key steps:

1. **Training with Data:** AI systems are fed vast amounts of data during their development phase. This data can include text, images, audio, or numerical datasets, depending on the AI's intended purpose. For example, an AI trained on millions of marketing campaigns will learn patterns and strategies that have historically led to success.

2. **Pattern Recognition:** Once trained, AI can identify patterns and correlations within new inputs. Unlike humans, who may overlook subtle connections due to cognitive biases or limited exposure, AI excels at uncovering trends across enormous datasets.

3. **Generating Outputs:** Using probabilistic models, AI generates outputs based on the patterns it has identified. For example, a natural language processing (NLP) model might predict the next word in a sentence or propose creative concepts based on a prompt.

4. **Iterative Refinement:** Advanced AI systems can refine their outputs through feedback loops. Users can rate or modify the AI's suggestions, helping the system improve over time.

AI Idea Generation in Action

AI generates ideas by synthesizing existing knowledge and extrapolating possibilities. Unlike human creativity, which is often driven by emotions, intuition, or cultural context, AI's creativity is rooted in data and logic. Here's how this plays out:

- **Combining Existing Concepts:** AI can merge unrelated ideas to create novel solutions. For instance, an AI tasked with brainstorming new product ideas might combine elements of sustainability and convenience, proposing a biodegradable coffee cup embedded with wildflower seeds.

- **Exploring Variations:** AI can produce numerous variations of a single idea, allowing users to explore a wide range of possibilities. For example, a marketing team might use AI to generate dozens of taglines for a campaign, each tailored to a different demographic.

- **Overcoming Human Limitations:** AI's ability to process vast amounts of data enables it to identify opportunities that humans might miss. For example, AI can analyze consumer behavior data to predict emerging trends and propose innovative products before competitors.

A Unique Approach to Creativity

AI's approach to creativity is fundamentally different from that of humans. While humans draw on lived experiences, cultural influences, and emotional connections, AI relies on data, algorithms, and probabilistic reasoning. This distinction is not a weakness but a strength. By complementing human creativity, AI opens new avenues for innovation.

For example, consider a team working on urban planning. The team brings their vision, values, and understanding of community needs to the table. AI, meanwhile, analyzes environmental data, traffic patterns, and historical trends to suggest practical, data-driven solutions. Together, they create a plan that balances human intuition with empirical insights.

Implications for Prompt Engineering

Understanding how AI thinks is crucial for crafting effective prompts. The quality of AI's output depends heavily on the clarity, context, and specificity of the input it receives. By framing prompts in a way that aligns with AI's strengths, users can maximize its creative potential.

For instance, instead of asking an AI to simply "generate ideas for a new app," a more effective prompt might specify the app's target audience, primary purpose, and unique features. This level of detail provides the AI with a clear framework, enabling it to deliver more relevant and actionable suggestions.

By understanding how AI thinks and generates ideas, we can move beyond viewing it as a mere tool and embrace it as a true creative partner. This partnership has the potential to redefine the boundaries of innovation, empowering us to tackle challenges with unprecedented creativity and precision.

The Difference Between Human and AI-Assisted Creativity

Human and AI-assisted creativity are distinct in their origins, processes, and outputs, but together they form a complementary partnership that enhances innovation.

1. Origin of Creativity

Human creativity stems from individual experiences, emotions, intuition, and cultural contexts. It often draws on abstract thinking and inspiration, leading to creations infused with personal meaning and emotional resonance. For example, an author might write a novel inspired by personal struggles or societal issues, creating a work that connects deeply with readers.

AI-assisted creativity, however, arises from data and algorithms. AI generates ideas by analyzing vast datasets and identifying patterns, relationships, and gaps. It lacks the emotional depth and subjective experiences of humans, but it excels at synthesizing knowledge and exploring possibilities that might elude human perception.

2. Idea Generation Process

Human creativity often follows a nonlinear path, involving brainstorming, trial and error, and moments of inspiration. It is shaped by emotions, collaboration, and sometimes serendipity.

AI operates systematically, processing inputs and generating outputs based on probabilities and patterns. For example, an AI system tasked with creating advertising slogans might analyze successful past campaigns to suggest ideas. While efficient, AI lacks the spontaneity and emotional triggers that characterize human ideation.

3. Strengths and Weaknesses

- **Human Creativity:**

  o **Strengths:** Emotional depth, originality, cultural relevance, and the ability to understand abstract or ambiguous ideas.

  o **Weaknesses:** Prone to cognitive biases, time-consuming, and limited by individual knowledge and energy.

- **AI-Assisted Creativity:**

  o **Strengths:** Speed, scalability, data-driven insights, and the ability to generate a high volume of ideas.

  o **Weaknesses:** No emotional understanding, reliance on the quality of training data, and a lack of intrinsic originality.

4. Collaboration Potential

AI and humans thrive when working together. AI can process data and generate numerous possibilities, serving as a creative catalyst, while humans filter, refine, and imbue these ideas with meaning, emotional resonance, and cultural sensitivity. For instance, a graphic designer might use AI to generate initial concepts for a campaign, then refine them to align with the intended message and audience.

By understanding these differences, we can effectively leverage AI as a creative partner, amplifying human ingenuity without diminishing its irreplaceable qualities. This symbiosis represents a new frontier in innovation.

Real-World Example: AI as a Creative Partner

The practical impact of AI as a creative partner is best illustrated through real-world examples, where collaboration between human ingenuity and AI-driven tools has led to remarkable outcomes. Let's explore a few scenarios across diverse industries to demonstrate the synergy.

1. Advertising and Marketing: Creating a Viral Campaign

A global beverage company wanted to create a campaign that resonated with Gen Z consumers. The team used AI to analyze trends, language patterns, and popular content on social media platforms.

- **How AI Contributed:** The AI identified key themes such as sustainability, self-expression, and nostalgia as appealing to the target audience. It then generated dozens of tagline options, visual concepts, and content ideas aligned with these themes.

- **How Humans Refined the Output:** The creative team selected and adapted the AI-generated ideas to fit the brand's tone and style. They designed an engaging campaign featuring short, nostalgic videos on TikTok and Instagram, which went viral, increasing brand engagement by 30%.

Key Insight: AI accelerated the brainstorming process, offering a range of starting points that humans polished and personalized, making the campaign authentic and relatable.

2. Product Design: Innovative Wearable Technology

An emerging tech company aimed to develop a smart fitness wearable that combined fashion with functionality. Using AI, the designers explored new possibilities.

- **How AI Contributed:** AI reviewed data from market surveys and competitor products, identifying unmet customer needs, such as better battery life, modular designs, and environmental sustainability. The system also suggested materials, features, and form factors based on customer feedback trends.

- **How Humans Refined the Output:** The design team used these insights to prototype a sleek, modular smartwatch that offered customizable bands and eco-friendly materials. AI-assisted testing further optimized the design for durability and performance.

Key Insight: AI's role in aggregating and analyzing customer feedback allowed designers to focus on creativity, resulting in a product that met market demand more effectively.

3. Film and Entertainment: Generating Story Concepts

In the entertainment industry, a screenwriter used AI to brainstorm ideas for a science-fiction screenplay.

- **How AI Contributed:** The writer input prompts such as "futuristic city," "ethical dilemmas," and "AI-human relationships." The system generated plot outlines, character sketches, and potential conflicts. It also analyzed the structures of successful sci-fi films, providing data-driven suggestions for pacing and story arcs.

- **How Humans Refined the Output:** The writer blended these ideas with personal experiences and creative vision, resulting in a screenplay that explored the moral complexities of a hyper-connected future.

Key Insight: AI provided inspiration and structure, but the emotional depth and philosophical nuances came from the writer's unique perspective.

4. Architecture: Designing a Sustainable Community

An architectural firm sought to design an eco-friendly housing development.

- **How AI Contributed:** AI modeled environmental impacts, suggested sustainable building materials, and simulated energy efficiency scenarios. It also generated innovative layouts that maximized natural light and ventilation while maintaining aesthetic appeal.

- **How Humans Refined the Output:** The architects incorporated these suggestions into a cohesive design, adding cultural elements to reflect the community's identity.

Key Insight: AI handled complex data analysis, enabling the architects to focus on creativity and cultural relevance.

These real-world examples showcase how AI serves as a powerful creative partner, offering efficiency, breadth, and inspiration, while humans provide the emotional depth, contextual understanding, and final touch needed to transform ideas into meaningful innovations. Together, they redefine what's possible in the creative process.

Actionable Insights for Readers

To fully harness AI as a creative partner, readers need practical strategies they can apply immediately. Here are actionable steps to integrate AI effectively into your creative workflows:

1. Start with Clear and Specific Prompts

The quality of AI output depends on the clarity of your input. Avoid vague prompts and instead provide context, desired outcomes, and constraints.

- **Example of a Weak Prompt:** "Generate ideas for a product."

- **Example of a Strong Prompt:** "Suggest innovative product ideas for eco-friendly, modular home furniture targeted at young urban professionals."

Tip: Experiment with different variations of the same prompt to explore diverse angles.

2. Use AI to Expand, Not Replace, Your Thinking

Approach AI as a collaborator that supplements your creativity rather than substituting it. Use AI to:

- Generate starting points or alternative perspectives.

- Explore data-driven insights that might challenge your assumptions.

- Combine AI-generated ideas with your intuition and expertise for a refined result.

  Example: If brainstorming ad slogans, use AI to generate multiple taglines, then tweak the output to align with your brand voice.

3. Iterate and Refine AI Output

AI's first response is rarely its best. Use it as a foundation to build upon:

- Identify the strongest elements of the AI's suggestions.

- Refine, reframe, or merge ideas to create something unique.

- Ask follow-up questions or adjust the prompt for deeper exploration.

  Tip: Iteration works best when paired with human judgment to ensure originality and relevance.

4. Combine Human Collaboration with AI Tools

AI shines as part of a team effort. Use it to facilitate brainstorming sessions by:

- Generating a pool of ideas to kickstart discussions.

- Offering a neutral, unbiased perspective to overcome groupthink.

- Helping teams align diverse viewpoints into cohesive strategies.

  Example: In a team brainstorming session, input collective ideas into an AI tool to identify patterns or gaps the group may have missed.

5. Leverage AI for Creative Block Breakthroughs

When you're stuck, let AI help reframe challenges or spark fresh inspiration. Use prompts that shift your perspective:

- "What are unconventional solutions to [problem]?"

- "Suggest a new angle for approaching [challenge]."

Example: A writer facing creative block can input "Generate ideas for unexpected plot twists in a thriller novel," letting AI trigger new directions.

6. Test and Validate Ideas with AI

Use AI not only for ideation but also to evaluate feasibility, risks, or scalability:

- Test different versions of a product idea or marketing pitch.

- Simulate scenarios to identify potential pitfalls.

Tip: Combine AI's analysis with your instincts and experience for well-rounded decision-making.

7. Develop a Workflow for AI Integration

Adopt a systematic approach to incorporating AI into your creative process:

1. **Define Goals:** Be clear about what you want to achieve (e.g., generating ideas, refining concepts, or testing strategies).

2. **Set Parameters:** Establish boundaries to guide AI's output (e.g., tone, audience, constraints).

3. **Evaluate Output:** Critically assess AI suggestions for relevance, originality, and alignment with your objectives.

4. **Iterate and Finalize:** Refine the ideas, combining AI's efficiency with your personal insights.

By following these steps, readers can turn AI from a simple tool into an indispensable creative partner, unlocking new possibilities in their personal and professional endeavors.

What Makes a Good Prompt?

In the rapidly evolving landscape of artificial intelligence, the ability to craft effective prompts is emerging as one of the most critical skills for harnessing AI's full potential. Prompts are not just questions or instructions; they are the foundation of every interaction with AI. Much like asking a well-thought-out question can unlock profound insights from an expert, a well-crafted prompt can draw out meaningful, creative, and actionable responses from AI systems.

Think of prompts as the language you use to converse with AI—a carefully constructed bridge that connects your intentions and the AI's output. A vague or poorly structured prompt often results in generic or irrelevant responses, wasting time and limiting the system's capabilities. Conversely, a clear, detailed, and context-rich prompt can transform a simple idea into a comprehensive solution or an innovative new perspective.

AI systems thrive on precision and guidance. While they excel at processing vast amounts of information and identifying patterns, they lack inherent intuition or understanding of ambiguous goals. That's where prompts come in. A good prompt gives the AI a clear starting point, provides context to guide its reasoning, and injects a touch of creativity to inspire novel solutions.

Beyond their functional purpose, prompts also empower users. They encourage us to think critically about the problems we aim to solve, the goals we want to achieve, and the questions we need answered. In crafting an effective prompt, we are compelled to clarify our own thinking, which often leads to deeper insights even before AI provides its output.

This chapter explores the art and science of prompt crafting, starting with the essential elements that make a prompt effective. Whether you're brainstorming new marketing strategies, solving complex organizational challenges, or developing innovative products, learning to design better prompts will elevate the quality of your results. By understanding and applying these principles, you'll unlock AI's potential as a true creative partner, rather than just a tool for automation.

Let's delve into what makes a prompt truly effective, how to distinguish weak prompts from strong ones, and how to refine your approach for maximum impact.

The Core Elements of a Good Prompt

A well-crafted prompt is the cornerstone of productive AI interactions. It's not enough to simply ask a question or give a command—the key lies in structuring the prompt in a way that guides the AI toward meaningful and actionable outputs. The following core elements—**clarity**, **context**, **creativity**, and **structure**—are essential for maximizing the effectiveness of your prompts.

1. Clarity: The Foundation of Understanding

Clarity is the most fundamental aspect of a good prompt. AI systems rely on explicit instructions, and vague or ambiguous prompts often result in generic or unhelpful responses.

- **What to Aim For:**

o Use precise language to avoid confusion.

o Define terms or concepts that may have multiple interpretations.

o Be concise while ensuring all critical details are included.

- **Example:**

o **Weak Prompt:** "Tell me about marketing strategies."

o **Strong Prompt:** "Explain three innovative digital marketing strategies for increasing social media engagement among 18-24-year-olds in the tech industry."

2. Context: Guiding the AI's Focus

AI thrives on context, which serves as the lens through which it processes your request. Providing relevant background information ensures that the response is tailored to your specific needs and avoids unnecessary generalities.

- **What to Aim For:**

o Offer the purpose or desired outcome of the prompt.

o Include specific parameters, such as timeframes, industries, or target audiences.

o Reference prior knowledge, if applicable, to maintain continuity in ongoing tasks.

- **Example:**

o **Weak Prompt:** "Suggest improvements for customer service."

o **Strong Prompt:** "Suggest three ways a mid-sized e-commerce company can improve its customer service during the holiday shopping season to reduce response times and enhance customer satisfaction."

3. Creativity: Inspiring Innovative Outputs

Adding an element of creativity to your prompt can encourage the AI to think beyond conventional solutions and generate unique ideas. This is especially important in brainstorming scenarios where innovation is the goal.

- **What to Aim For:**

o Phrase prompts as open-ended questions to encourage exploration.

o Challenge the AI to approach the problem from multiple angles or perspectives.

o Use hypothetical scenarios to inspire unconventional thinking.

- **Example:**

o **Weak Prompt:** "List some features for a fitness app."

- o **Strong Prompt:** "Imagine a fitness app designed for users with busy schedules who struggle to find motivation. What unique features could help them stay consistent and engaged?"

4. Structure: Organizing for Maximum Impact

How you structure your prompt can significantly influence the quality and usability of the AI's response. Breaking down complex prompts into smaller, digestible components allows the AI to focus on each aspect systematically.

- **What to Aim For:**

- o Use bullet points or numbered lists to outline multiple questions or tasks.

- o Specify the format of the response (e.g., a list, paragraphs, or step-by-step instructions).

- o Avoid overloading the prompt with too many unrelated elements.

- **Example:**

- o **Weak Prompt:** "Give me tips for leadership."

- o **Strong Prompt:**
  "Provide leadership tips for:

1. Building trust with a new team.

2. Managing conflicts between team members.

3. Motivating employees during challenging times."

Bringing It All Together

When clarity, context, creativity, and structure are combined, they create a prompt that is not only easy for the AI to interpret but also ensures that the output is relevant, actionable, and insightful. By mastering these core elements, you'll be equipped to extract the full potential of AI for brainstorming, problem-solving, and beyond.

Weak vs. Strong Prompts: Breaking It Down

Crafting effective prompts is a skill that can transform your interaction with AI. Weak prompts often result in generic or irrelevant outputs, while strong prompts can produce precise, actionable, and innovative responses. This section compares weak and strong prompts across various scenarios, showing how small adjustments can significantly improve outcomes.

What Defines a Weak Prompt?

Weak prompts lack clarity, context, or specificity. They often:

- Fail to provide enough detail for the AI to generate meaningful insights.

- Use ambiguous language that leads to generic or off-topic responses.

- Omit clear instructions on the format or focus of the output.

What Defines a Strong Prompt?

Strong prompts, on the other hand, are:

- **Clear:** They leave no room for misinterpretation.

- **Contextual:** They provide the necessary background or constraints to guide the AI's reasoning.

- **Creative:** They encourage exploration and innovation when needed.

- **Well-Structured:** They break complex tasks into manageable parts or specify the desired format of the response.

Side-by-Side Examples of Weak vs. Strong Prompts

1. Scenario: Generating Marketing Ideas

- **Weak Prompt:**
  "Give me ideas for marketing a product."

- **Why It's Weak:**

  o Lacks clarity about the product or target audience.

  o Does not specify the type of marketing ideas needed (e.g., digital campaigns, social media strategies).

- **Strong Prompt:**
  "Suggest five creative marketing strategies for a new eco-friendly water bottle targeting young professionals aged 25-35. Focus on social media campaigns and partnerships with influencers."

- **Why It's Strong:**

  o Provides context (eco-friendly water bottle, young professionals).

  o Specifies the desired type of strategies (social media and influencer partnerships).

  o Sets a clear expectation for the output (five strategies).

  2. Scenario: Problem-Solving in Team Management

- **Weak Prompt:**

  "How can I improve team performance?"

- **Why It's Weak:**

o Broad and unspecific—does not clarify the team's challenges or context.

- **Strong Prompt:**

  "My team is struggling with meeting deadlines due to poor communication. Suggest three practical strategies to improve communication and ensure better time management."

- **Why It's Strong:**

o Identifies the specific challenge (poor communication affecting deadlines).

o Sets a clear goal (improving communication and time management).

o Limits the scope to three actionable strategies.

3. Scenario: Product Development Brainstorming

- **Weak Prompt:**

  "What should I add to my app?"

- **Why It's Weak:**

o Vague and lacks any details about the app or its users.

- **Strong Prompt:**

  "My fitness app focuses on helping users track their workouts and progress. Suggest three unique features that could motivate users to stay consistent, such as gamification or social engagement tools."

- **Why It's Strong:**

- Provides the app's purpose (tracking workouts and progress).

- Targets specific outcomes (motivation and consistency).

- Mentions examples to inspire creativity (gamification, social engagement tools).

4. Scenario: Writing Content

- **Weak Prompt:**
  "Write a blog post introduction."

- **Why It's Weak:**

- Does not specify the blog's topic, tone, or audience.

- **Strong Prompt:**
  "Write a compelling introduction for a blog post about the benefits of remote work for small business owners. Highlight increased productivity and cost savings while maintaining a professional yet conversational tone."

- **Why It's Strong:**

- Clearly defines the topic (benefits of remote work for small businesses).

- Specifies the key points to focus on (productivity, cost savings).

- Guides the tone of the response (professional yet conversational).

Analyzing the AI Outputs

For each example, the strong prompt would generate outputs that:

- Are relevant and tailored to the specific context.

- Contain actionable insights or ideas.

- Require minimal refinement, saving time and effort.

  Weak prompts, in contrast, often produce outputs that are:

- Generic or overly broad.

- Not aligned with the user's goals.

- Less useful, requiring additional clarification or re-prompting.

Tips for Strengthening Prompts

1. **Be Specific:** Clearly state what you want the AI to deliver. Avoid vague language.

2. **Provide Context:** Include any relevant background information, constraints, or examples.

3. **Limit Scope:** Narrow the focus to prevent overly broad or diluted responses.

4. **Iterate:** Experiment with rephrasing and refining prompts to improve outputs.

By understanding the difference between weak and strong prompts and applying these principles, you'll unlock the full potential of AI for brainstorming, problem-solving, and content creation.

Prompt Crafting Techniques

Crafting effective prompts is an art and science that enables you to extract the most valuable insights from AI. By employing proven techniques, you can consistently produce results that are clear, relevant, and actionable.

These techniques focus on structuring prompts to align with your goals while encouraging the AI to deliver its best performance.

1. Be Specific and Explicit

A specific prompt minimizes ambiguity and ensures the AI understands exactly what you're asking. Explicit details about the task, format, and desired outcomes guide the AI to generate focused and relevant responses.

- **Example:**
  - **Vague Prompt:** "Tell me about leadership."
  - **Specific Prompt:** "Explain five key traits of effective leadership in the context of managing remote teams."

2. Use Context to Anchor the AI's Response

Providing context frames the problem and gives the AI a point of reference for its response. This can include background information, the intended audience, or the problem's scope.

- **Example:**
  - **Without Context:** "Suggest a new feature for my app."
  - **With Context:** "My app is designed for freelancers to manage their projects and invoices. Suggest one feature that could enhance time-tracking capabilities."

3. Break Down Complex Requests

For multifaceted tasks, breaking the prompt into smaller components ensures clarity and improves the AI's ability to address each part thoroughly. Use bullet points or numbered lists to structure the request.

- **Example:**

o **Overloaded Prompt:** "Tell me how to improve my business strategy and attract more customers."

o **Broken-Down Prompt:**
"1. Suggest three ways to improve a small business's marketing strategy.
2. Provide two ideas for attracting repeat customers."

4. Experiment with Open-Ended and Close-Ended Prompts

- **Open-Ended Prompts** are great for brainstorming and generating ideas:

o **Example:** "What innovative solutions can help reduce food waste in urban areas?"

- **Close-Ended Prompts** work well for specific answers or when seeking actionable advice:

o **Example:** "List five technologies that can track food waste in restaurants."

5. Incorporate Creative Framing

Reframe the problem in a way that encourages the AI to think innovatively. Hypothetical scenarios or role-playing prompts can stimulate unconventional ideas.

- **Example:**

o "Imagine you're designing a product for a Mars colony. What features would be essential for a communication device?"

6. Specify the Desired Output Format

Guide the AI by clearly stating how you want the response formatted. This is particularly useful for structured outputs like lists, summaries, or step-by-step instructions.

- **Example:**

o "Summarize the following article in three bullet points."

o "Provide a step-by-step guide to creating a content marketing strategy."

7. Use Constraints to Sharpen Focus

Adding constraints helps the AI deliver targeted responses within defined boundaries. Constraints can include word limits, timeframes, industries, or demographic targets.

- **Example:**

o "Write a 150-word social media post promoting a new sustainable clothing brand."

o "Suggest budget-friendly marketing ideas for a small nonprofit organization."

8. Iterate for Refinement

Don't hesitate to refine and adjust your prompts based on the AI's initial output. Feedback loops allow you to fine-tune the request for improved results.

- **Technique:**

  o Start with a general prompt: "How can I improve my product design?"

  o Refine based on the response: "Focus on design improvements that appeal to Gen Z users in the gaming industry."

9. Leverage Analogies and Comparisons

Encourage creative problem-solving by prompting the AI to draw analogies or comparisons. This can lead to innovative ideas that are inspired by different domains.

- **Example:**

  o "What lessons can a small coffee shop learn from the customer experience strategies of tech giants like Apple?"

10. Ask "What If" Questions

"What if" prompts stimulate exploration of new possibilities or alternative approaches, opening the door to creative solutions.

- **Example:**

  o "What if public transportation systems were designed like subscription-based streaming services? How could this improve accessibility?"

Applying These Techniques

By employing these techniques, you can craft prompts that maximize the potential of AI. Strong prompts not only improve the relevance and quality of responses but also help streamline workflows and unlock innovative solutions.

Real-World Applications of Effective Prompt Crafting

Crafting effective prompts has practical applications across industries and roles, enabling individuals and teams to solve problems, generate ideas, and streamline processes. Below are examples of how prompt crafting can be applied in different real-world scenarios, illustrating its impact and versatility.

1. Marketing and Branding

AI can help marketers generate creative campaigns, refine branding strategies, and tailor messages for specific audiences through effective prompts.

- **Scenario:** Creating an Ad Campaign

  o **Prompt:** "Generate three creative ad ideas for a new vegan protein bar targeting health-conscious millennials. Focus on humor and emphasize sustainability."

  o **Output:** Ideas include a humorous social media video series showing "meat-eaters going vegan overnight" after trying the bar and slogans like "Snack Smart, Snack Green."

- **Impact:** Saves time in brainstorming sessions, providing a foundation for further refinement.

2. Product Development

AI supports product innovation by identifying customer pain points and suggesting potential solutions.

- **Scenario:** Enhancing an Existing Product

o **Prompt:** "Suggest two unique features for a fitness app that tracks workouts and motivates users through social engagement."

o **Output:** Recommendations for a "friendly competition leaderboard" and "weekly community challenges with virtual rewards."

- **Impact:** Encourages fresh ideas that align with user engagement trends.

3. Team Management

HR professionals and managers can use AI to address challenges like improving communication or fostering collaboration.

- **Scenario:** Addressing Team Dynamics

o **Prompt:** "My remote team struggles with miscommunication. Provide three practical strategies to improve collaboration and ensure everyone stays on the same page."

o **Output:** Suggestions such as implementing a shared task board, scheduling weekly alignment meetings, and using concise messaging templates.

- **Impact:** Provides actionable advice tailored to specific team challenges.

4. Education and Training

Educators can leverage AI to create tailored learning experiences, develop engaging content, and explore new teaching strategies.

- **Scenario:** Designing a Lesson Plan

- Prompt: "Create a one-hour interactive lesson plan on climate change for high school students. Include a group activity and discussion prompts."

- Output: A detailed lesson plan with an icebreaker quiz, group activity building a "climate action plan," and discussion topics like renewable energy solutions.

- Impact: Saves educators time while enhancing lesson creativity and engagement.

5. Strategic Planning

AI can assist business leaders in scenario planning, market analysis, and risk assessment.

- Scenario: Identifying Market Opportunities

- Prompt: "Analyze potential growth opportunities for a mid-sized software company specializing in cybersecurity. Suggest three new market segments to target."

- Output: Suggestions to explore the healthcare sector for patient data protection, small businesses needing affordable solutions, and government contracts for national infrastructure security.

- Impact: Expands strategic thinking by highlighting new directions.

6. Content Creation

Content creators and writers can rely on AI to overcome writer's block, brainstorm topics, and refine drafts.

- Scenario: Writing a Blog Post

o **Prompt:** "Draft an outline for a 1,000-word blog post titled 'The Future of Remote Work in Creative Industries.' Include three key sections with subtopics."

o **Output:** A clear structure with sections like "Emerging Trends in Remote Creativity," "Challenges and Solutions," and "The Role of Technology in Remote Collaboration."

- **Impact:** Provides a solid starting point for content creation.

7. Problem-Solving in Healthcare

Healthcare professionals can use AI to explore solutions for patient care, operational efficiency, and public health campaigns.

- **Scenario:** Improving Patient Retention

o **Prompt:** "Suggest three strategies for a small dental clinic to improve patient retention rates."

o **Output:** Strategies include sending personalized appointment reminders, offering loyalty discounts, and providing value-added services like free whitening for long-term patients.

- **Impact:** Delivers actionable strategies to enhance patient satisfaction and loyalty.

8. Creative Collaboration

AI enhances brainstorming sessions by acting as a neutral contributor, generating diverse perspectives.

- **Scenario:** Collaborative Problem-Solving

- o **Prompt:** "Facilitate a brainstorming session for a team of software developers to improve user engagement on a gaming platform. Provide discussion points and initial ideas."

- o **Output:** Discussion topics like gamification, user rewards, and daily challenges, along with example ideas such as "seasonal events with exclusive rewards."

- **Impact:** Aligns team members with a starting point for innovation.

Key Benefits of Prompt Crafting in Real-World Applications

1. **Time Efficiency:** Reduces the time spent on initial ideation or research.

2. **Enhanced Creativity:** Encourages fresh and innovative ideas.

3. **Tailored Solutions:** Generates responses tailored to specific needs or challenges.

4. **Scalability:** Applicable across industries, roles, and levels of complexity.

By leveraging the power of effective prompts, professionals across industries can unlock new opportunities, improve workflows, and tackle challenges with greater confidence.

Interactive Exercise: Crafting Better Prompts

This exercise will help you practice and refine your skills in crafting effective AI prompts. By experimenting with different structures, adding clarity, context, and creativity, you'll gain confidence in using AI as a collaborative tool.

Objective

To create strong, effective prompts tailored to different scenarios, evaluate the AI's response, and refine your prompts for improved results.

Step 1: Start with a Simple Prompt

Begin with a basic or vague prompt and identify its limitations.

1. Write a simple prompt.

o **Example:** "Suggest ideas for a marketing campaign."

2. Analyze the AI's response.

o Is the response clear and useful?

o Are the ideas relevant to your specific needs?

3. Note the weaknesses of the prompt (e.g., lack of context, unclear goals).

Step 2: Add Clarity

Refine your prompt by being more specific about your goals or requirements.

1. Rewrite the prompt to include clarity.

o **Example:** "Suggest three creative marketing campaign ideas for a new eco-friendly water bottle targeting young adults."

2. Compare the AI's new response to the original.

o Does it better address your needs?

o   Are the ideas more actionable or targeted?

Step 3: Introduce Context

Context helps frame the AI's response and ensures it aligns with your objectives.

1.   Revise the prompt to add background or context.

o   **Example:** "Our eco-friendly water bottle is made of 100% recycled materials and features a sleek design. It is priced mid-range and appeals to environmentally conscious young professionals. Suggest three creative marketing campaign ideas."

2.   Review the updated response.

o   Is it more aligned with your brand or goals?

Step 4: Use Constraints or Formatting Guidance

Incorporate constraints or specify the desired format for the response.

1.   Add a word limit, tone, or format.

o   **Example:** "Generate three creative marketing campaign ideas for an eco-friendly water bottle. Each idea should be under 50 words and include a tagline."

2.   Assess whether the AI followed the constraints and improved its output.

Step 5: Experiment with Creativity and Hypotheticals

Challenge the AI to think outside the box by framing prompts creatively or as hypotheticals.

1. Add creative framing.

o **Example:** "Imagine you are a marketing expert at an innovative startup. Suggest three out-of-the-box marketing campaigns for an eco-friendly water bottle targeting Gen Z consumers."

2. Evaluate the results for creativity and originality.

Step 6: Iterate and Refine

Continue adjusting your prompts based on the AI's output and your goals. Use feedback loops to sharpen clarity, context, and specificity.

- **Refined Prompt Example:**
  "We're launching an eco-friendly water bottle made of 100% recycled materials. It's sleek, affordable, and aimed at environmentally conscious young professionals. Generate three creative marketing campaigns that incorporate humor and focus on sustainability. Each idea should include a tagline and a brief description (under 50 words)."

Guided Reflection

After completing the exercise, reflect on the following:

1. How did refining your prompts improve the AI's responses?

2. What strategies helped you achieve clarity, context, and creativity in your prompts?

3. How might you apply these techniques in your own professional or personal projects?

Advanced Challenge

For those ready to level up:

1. Use AI to critique and improve your prompt.

o **Prompt Example:** "Analyze this prompt: 'Suggest ideas for a marketing campaign.' How can it be improved to get more specific and actionable responses?"

2. Implement the AI's suggestions and compare the outcomes.

   By practicing these steps, you'll develop a systematic approach to crafting better prompts, unlocking the full potential of AI in your creative and problem-solving processes.

Common Mistakes and How to Avoid Them in Crafting Prompts

Crafting effective AI prompts is both an art and a science. While the process may seem straightforward, certain pitfalls can limit the quality of the AI's output. By identifying these common mistakes and learning how to avoid them, you can maximize the value of AI in brainstorming and problem-solving.

1. Being Too Vague

Mistake:
Providing prompts that are overly broad or lack specifics, leading to generic or irrelevant responses.

- **Example of a Weak Prompt:**
  "Give me ideas for a business."

- **Why It's a Problem:**

  The lack of clarity makes it difficult for the AI to tailor its response to your needs, resulting in superficial suggestions.

  Solution:

  Add specificity by including details about the industry, target audience, or desired outcomes.

- **Improved Prompt:**

  "Suggest three innovative business ideas in the wellness industry for urban professionals aged 25-40, focusing on mental health and self-care."

2. Omitting Context

Mistake:

Failing to provide background information or the purpose of the prompt, leading to irrelevant or misaligned results.

- **Example of a Weak Prompt:**

  "Write a blog post introduction."

- **Why It's a Problem:**

  Without context, the AI has no understanding of the blog's audience, tone, or topic.

  Solution:

  Include context to guide the AI's response.

- **Improved Prompt:**

  "Write a 150-word introduction for a blog post targeting small business owners. The topic is how to use social media to attract local customers, with a friendly and practical tone."

3. Ignoring Tone and Style

Mistake:

Neglecting to specify the tone or style of the output, resulting in responses that don't match your intended voice.

- **Example of a Weak Prompt:**
  "Explain blockchain technology."

- **Why It's a Problem:**
  The AI may provide a response that is too technical, casual, or formal, depending on its default assumptions.

  Solution:
  Specify the desired tone or audience.

- **Improved Prompt:**
  "Explain blockchain technology in simple terms, as if you're teaching a beginner with no technical background."

4. Overloading the Prompt

Mistake:

Including too many instructions or questions in a single prompt, overwhelming the AI and causing unclear or fragmented results.

- **Example of a Weak Prompt:**
  "Explain blockchain technology, discuss its advantages, list five use cases, and give examples of companies using it."

- **Why It's a Problem:**

  The AI might struggle to prioritize the requests or produce responses that lack depth.

  Solution:

  Break down complex prompts into smaller, focused ones.

- **Improved Prompts:**

  o "Explain blockchain technology in simple terms."

  o "List five advantages of blockchain technology."

  o "Provide examples of companies using blockchain technology and their use cases."

5. Not Iterating or Refining

Mistake:

Using the first AI-generated response without reviewing or refining the prompt for better results.

- **Example of a Weak Approach:**

  Accepting a generic list of ideas and moving forward without further input.

- **Why It's a Problem:**

  The initial response may miss nuances or fail to explore deeper insights.

  Solution:

  Iterate by refining the prompt or asking follow-up questions.

- **Improved Process:**

- First Prompt: "Suggest three creative marketing ideas for a new fitness app."

- Refined Prompt: "Suggest three creative marketing ideas for a fitness app targeting women aged 30-50, focusing on convenience and community-building."

6. Over-Reliance on AI

Mistake:
Expecting the AI to provide fully-formed solutions without human input or critical thinking.

- **Why It's a Problem:**
AI lacks the emotional intelligence, creativity, and contextual awareness that humans bring to decision-making.

- **Solution:**
Use AI as a collaborator rather than a replacement, and review its outputs critically.

- **Action:**
Treat AI-generated ideas as a starting point to build upon, refine, and adapt to your needs.

7. Ignoring the AI's Limitations

Mistake:
Asking the AI for tasks beyond its capabilities, such as highly subjective opinions or access to current events.

- **Example of a Weak Prompt:**
"What's the best movie to watch tonight?"

- **Why It's a Problem:**

  AI cannot account for personal tastes or real-time recommendations.

  Solution:

  Frame prompts to focus on general suggestions or guidance.

- **Improved Prompt:**

  "List five critically acclaimed movies in the comedy genre suitable for a family audience."

8. Forgetting to Specify the Desired Output Format

Mistake:

Not defining how you want the response to be presented, leading to unstructured or less useful results.

- **Example of a Weak Prompt:**

  "Summarize this report."

- **Why It's a Problem:**

  The AI may not know whether to write a detailed summary, bullet points, or a brief overview.

  Solution:

  Specify the format.

- **Improved Prompt:**

  "Summarize this report in three bullet points highlighting key insights."

  How to Avoid These Pitfalls

1. **Start with a Clear Goal:** Define what you need from the AI and structure the prompt accordingly.

2. **Iterate and Experiment:** Treat prompt crafting as an iterative process. Refine prompts based on the AI's initial response.

3. **Provide Context:** The more information you provide, the better the AI can align its output with your needs.

4. **Specify the Format:** Clearly state how you want the information to be presented (e.g., lists, paragraphs, steps).

5. **Balance Complexity:** Be detailed but avoid overloading the prompt.

By recognizing these common mistakes and adopting best practices, you'll become more adept at crafting prompts that yield insightful, actionable, and high-quality responses from AI. This foundation will empower you to unlock AI's full potential in your personal and professional endeavors.

Building a Habit of Effective Prompting

Developing the skill of effective prompting is not a one-time task—it's a habit that can be cultivated through practice, reflection, and continuous improvement. Much like learning to communicate clearly with a human collaborator, crafting strong prompts requires an intentional approach to maximize AI's potential as a creative and problem-solving partner.

1. Understand Your AI Tool

The first step in building effective prompting habits is understanding the capabilities and limitations of the AI you're working with. Different AI tools may excel in certain areas, such as language generation, data analysis, or creative brainstorming.

- **Actionable Step:** Explore the tool's documentation and features to gain insight into its strengths and constraints. This will help you craft prompts that align with its capabilities.

- **Example Habit:** Before starting any session, spend a few minutes considering how the tool can specifically assist with your task.

2. Start Simple, Then Iterate

Effective prompting often begins with simplicity. Instead of trying to craft the perfect prompt immediately, start with a straightforward question or instruction and refine based on the AI's initial response.

- **Actionable Step:** Begin with a broad prompt, then narrow your focus in subsequent iterations.

- **Example Habit:** Build a "prompt refinement loop" where each response informs your next question.

o **Initial Prompt:** "Suggest ideas for a new marketing campaign."

o **Refined Prompt:** "Suggest ideas for a social media campaign targeting Gen Z, focusing on eco-friendly products."

3. Adopt a Consistent Structure

Creating prompts that follow a clear structure can improve the quality of AI responses. A consistent framework ensures that your instructions are both comprehensive and easy to follow.

- **Actionable Step:** Use the "C3 Formula" for prompts:

o **Clarity:** Be precise about what you're asking.

o **Context:** Provide relevant background information.

o **Creativity:** Encourage innovative or diverse thinking.

- **Example Habit:** Regularly use templates to structure your prompts.

o **Template:** "Generate [output type] for [audience] about [topic], with a tone/style that is [specific tone/style]."

4. Practice Active Reflection

After each interaction, take time to review the AI's response. Identify what worked well and where the prompt could be improved. This reflection builds your awareness of effective strategies.

- **Actionable Step:** Maintain a "Prompt Journal" to document your successful and unsuccessful prompts.

- **Example Habit:** After using a prompt, note down:

o What elements led to a strong response?

o What could be clarified or adjusted next time?

5. Experiment with Creativity

AI thrives on creative and unconventional prompts. Building a habit of experimenting with different approaches can unlock unexpected insights and ideas.

- **Actionable Step:** Try prompts that use metaphors, analogies, or hypothetical scenarios.

- **Example Habit:** Dedicate time each week to experiment with "out-of-the-box" prompts.

o **Example:** "Describe how launching a new app is like planning a space mission. Suggest strategies based on this analogy."

6. Balance Precision and Flexibility

While precision is critical, overly rigid prompts can stifle the AI's creativity. Learn to strike a balance by providing enough detail while leaving room for the AI to explore diverse interpretations.

- **Actionable Step:** Test prompts with varying levels of specificity to see how they affect the output.

- **Example Habit:** Create two versions of the same prompt—one highly specific and one broader—and compare the results.

7. Make Prompting a Routine

Integrating prompting into your regular workflow ensures that you consistently practice and refine the skill. The more you engage with AI, the more intuitive and effective your prompts will become.

- **Actionable Step:** Set aside dedicated time for prompt crafting and experimentation as part of your daily or weekly schedule.

- **Example Habit:** Start each workday by crafting AI prompts for your top three priorities.

8. Collaborate with Others

Learning from others' prompting techniques can provide new perspectives and ideas. Sharing and discussing prompts within a team can lead to collective improvement.

- **Actionable Step:** Create a shared document or workspace where team members can contribute their best prompts and techniques.

- **Example Habit:** Hold monthly brainstorming sessions focused on improving the team's prompting skills.

9. Learn from Feedback

AI-generated outputs are a form of feedback that helps you understand how well your prompt worked. Use this feedback to iteratively refine your technique.

- **Actionable Step:** Treat AI responses as data points. Analyze what aspects of the response align with your expectations and what doesn't.

- **Example Habit:** For each response, ask yourself, "What could I have added or removed from the prompt to get closer to my goal?"

10. Stay Curious and Open to Growth

The world of AI is constantly evolving, and so is the art of prompting. Cultivate a mindset of curiosity and a willingness to adapt your habits as you discover new techniques.

- **Actionable Step:** Follow updates, best practices, and case studies related to AI prompting.

- **Example Habit:** Commit to learning one new prompting technique or strategy each month.

Building a Lifelong Skill

By cultivating habits like reflection, experimentation, and continuous learning, you can master the art of effective prompting. These habits not only improve your ability to interact with AI but also enhance your critical thinking and problem-solving skills in broader contexts. Over time, prompting will become an intuitive and indispensable tool in your creative and professional toolkit.

Part 2: Applications of AI Brainstorming

The Landscape of Innovation Today

Innovation is often seen as the lifeblood of thriving businesses, driving growth, competitiveness, and relevance in fast-paced markets. Traditionally, brainstorming sessions, market surveys, and focus groups have been the primary tools for generating ideas and refining products. While these methods have brought countless breakthroughs, they often fall short in today's rapidly evolving landscape.

The challenges are clear:

- **Time-Intensive Processes:** Gathering and analyzing market data manually can take weeks, leaving businesses lagging behind competitors.

- **Limited Perspectives:** Even the most diverse teams bring inherent biases and blind spots to the table.

- **Data Overload:** The sheer volume of information available today can overwhelm decision-makers, leading to analysis paralysis.

Enter **Artificial Intelligence**—a transformative force reshaping how we approach innovation.

Why AI Is a Game-Changer for Creativity

AI has transcended its role as a tool for automation, becoming a partner in creativity and problem-solving. By leveraging vast datasets, natural language processing, and predictive analytics, AI can process information at speeds unimaginable to humans. More importantly, it can surface connections and opportunities that may otherwise go unnoticed.

Key advantages of AI in innovation include:

1. **Scalability:** AI can analyze massive amounts of market data, from customer reviews to competitor strategies, in minutes.

2. **Unbiased Insights:** Unlike human teams, AI approaches problems without preconceived notions or emotional biases.

3. **Rapid Iteration:** AI enables businesses to quickly test, refine, and pivot ideas based on real-time feedback.

4. **Endless Creativity:** AI thrives on combining disparate elements into unique solutions, often offering unexpected ideas.

Imagine using AI to identify untapped niches in the pet care industry, predict consumer trends in renewable energy, or design the next big feature for your software product—all within hours.

From Ideas to Impact: The Role of Prompt Engineering

At the heart of harnessing AI for innovation lies a crucial skill: **prompt engineering**. Crafting the right prompts transforms vague, uninspiring ideas into actionable insights. Think of prompts as the questions that guide AI's exploration—when framed effectively, they unlock the full potential of AI as a creative partner.

For example:

- A weak prompt: *"What are some product ideas for healthcare?"*

- A strong prompt: *"Identify three innovative product ideas for wearable health devices that cater to people over 50 and focus on preventative care."*

Through this chapter, we'll explore how to rethink the innovation process with AI, shifting from traditional brainstorming methods to a more dynamic, data-driven, and creative approach. By mastering the art of asking the right questions, you'll unlock the potential to:

- **Identify unmet needs** in the market.

- **Generate novel ideas** that resonate with target audiences.

- **Refine products** for maximum impact and value.

A New Era of Innovation

This isn't just about embracing a tool—it's about adopting a mindset. AI empowers businesses to innovate faster, smarter, and with greater confidence. As we delve deeper, you'll see how this partnership between human creativity and AI's analytical power can revolutionize your approach to product and service development.

Let's rethink innovation together, with AI as your guide.

Identifying Gaps in the Market

In a world where consumer needs evolve rapidly and industries face constant disruption, identifying gaps in the market is no longer optional—it's essential for survival and growth. This is where Artificial Intelligence (AI) excels, offering a fresh perspective on market analysis that surpasses traditional methods.

Why Finding Gaps Matters

Market gaps represent opportunities—unmet needs, underserved audiences, or problems waiting for solutions. Identifying and acting on these gaps can:

1. **Create Differentiation:** Stand out in crowded markets by offering something unique.

2. **Drive Customer Loyalty:** Address needs that competitors have overlooked.

3. **Enable Growth:** Expand into untapped niches and gain a first-mover advantage.

However, pinpointing these gaps often requires combing through vast amounts of data—consumer feedback, industry reports, competitor offerings, and emerging trends. This is where AI proves invaluable.

How AI Identifies Market Gaps

AI can process and analyze datasets that would overwhelm even the most experienced market researchers. Here's how it helps:

1. **Analyzing Customer Feedback at Scale**
   AI tools can process millions of customer reviews, social media posts, and survey responses to identify recurring pain points and unmet expectations.

o **Example Prompt:**
   "Analyze 10,000 customer reviews of wearable fitness devices to identify the top three unmet needs or complaints."

2. **Comparing Competitor Offerings**

   AI can map competitor products, features, and pricing to highlight gaps in the market.

   o **Example Prompt:**

   "Compare the features of the top 5 meal delivery services in the U.S. and suggest areas where they are lacking in convenience or sustainability."

3. **Spotting Emerging Trends**

   AI's ability to process real-time data allows it to detect shifts in consumer behavior and predict upcoming trends before they become mainstream.

   o **Example Prompt:**

   "Analyze social media trends in renewable energy products over the last year to identify emerging consumer interests."

4. **Segmenting Underserved Audiences**

   AI can segment audiences based on demographics, preferences, or behaviors to identify groups that current offerings fail to serve.

   o **Example Prompt:**

   "Identify underserved customer segments in the outdoor apparel market and suggest product ideas tailored to their needs."

Real-World Example: AI in Action

A mid-sized tech company wanted to launch a new smart home device but was unsure how to differentiate it. Using AI-driven analysis, they discovered that many consumers were frustrated with the complexity of existing devices. By focusing on simplicity and ease of use, they developed a voice-activated device with a user-friendly interface, which became a bestseller in its category.

Practical Steps to Use AI for Identifying Market Gaps

1. **Define Your Focus Area:** Start with a clear idea of the market or problem you want to explore.

2. **Craft Precise Prompts:** Use specific, actionable language in your AI queries to direct its analysis.

3. **Validate Findings:** Use AI's insights as a starting point, then validate them with human expertise and additional research.

4. **Iterate and Refine:** Continuously refine prompts and hypotheses as new data emerges.

Empowering Innovation Through Market Gaps

AI doesn't just help you find market gaps—it enables you to address them with confidence. By identifying unmet needs and underserved audiences, businesses can innovate in ways that resonate deeply with consumers.

Ready to discover how AI can turn market gaps into opportunities? The next section will dive into crafting prompts that generate groundbreaking ideas for products and services.

Generating New Product Ideas

Once you've identified gaps in the market, the next step is to generate innovative ideas to fill those gaps. Artificial Intelligence (AI) can be a game-changing partner in this process, not only speeding up ideation but also expanding the creative boundaries of what's possible. By leveraging AI's pattern recognition, predictive analytics, and natural language processing capabilities, you can move from vague concepts to actionable, market-ready product ideas.

The Role of AI in Product Ideation

AI serves as an amplifier for human creativity by:

1. **Generating a High Volume of Ideas:** AI can brainstorm dozens of potential solutions based on a single prompt, giving you more options to explore.

2. **Providing Unique Perspectives:** AI's approach to combining unrelated concepts can lead to fresh and unexpected ideas.

3. **Simulating Market Reactions:** AI can predict how target audiences might respond to different product ideas, helping refine concepts early.

How AI Helps Generate Product Ideas

1. **Combining Existing Concepts into New Innovations**
   AI excels at synthesizing disparate ideas into new combinations.

o **Example Prompt:**
   "Generate 10 innovative product ideas by combining smart home technology with sustainable materials."

2. **Adapting Features to Solve Consumer Pain Points**
   AI can use customer feedback and market analysis to suggest product features tailored to specific needs.

o **Example Prompt:**
   "Based on customer reviews of fitness trackers, suggest three new features to improve user experience for beginners."

3. **Exploring Adjacent Markets**

   AI can identify opportunities to apply proven solutions from one market to another.

   o **Example Prompt:**

   "Analyze trends in subscription-based entertainment services and suggest how they can be applied to the pet care industry."

4. **Scenario-Based Ideation**

   AI can simulate "what if" scenarios to explore how changes in technology or consumer behavior might create opportunities for new products.

   o **Example Prompt:**

   "Imagine a future where electric vehicles dominate the market. What new products or services might emerge to support this transition?"

Framework for Generating Product Ideas with AI

1. **Start with Clear Objectives**

   Define the problem or market gap you want to address. For example, "How can we create eco-friendly alternatives to single-use plastics?"

2. **Craft Precise Prompts**

   Use structured prompts that guide AI toward relevant outputs.

   o **Weak Prompt:**

   "Suggest some new product ideas."

   o **Strong Prompt:**

   "Generate three innovative ideas for reusable packaging solutions targeted at environmentally conscious millennials."

3. **Refine and Filter Ideas**

   Use AI to evaluate and refine the initial list of ideas based on feasibility, cost, and market fit.

o **Example Prompt:**

   "Assess the scalability and cost-effectiveness of these three product ideas and rank them."

4. **Iterate Through Feedback**

   Combine AI-generated ideas with team input and real-world feedback to refine your concepts further.

Case Study: AI Driving Product Innovation

A small beverage company wanted to create a new line of functional drinks. Using AI to analyze health trends and consumer preferences, they discovered a growing interest in beverages that promote cognitive health. Based on AI-generated suggestions, they developed a nootropic-infused sparkling water with minimal sugar, which resonated with health-conscious millennials and quickly gained market traction.

Tips for Effective AI-Driven Ideation

1. **Be Specific:** Narrow your prompts to a particular problem, market, or demographic to get focused results.

2. **Encourage Creativity:** Experiment with "blue-sky" prompts that allow AI to propose unconventional solutions.

3. **Incorporate Constraints:** Define parameters like budget, materials, or timeline to ensure ideas are practical.

o   **Example Prompt:**

"Suggest low-cost product ideas for the travel accessories market using materials under $10 per unit."

4. **Use AI Iteratively:** Run multiple prompts, combining and refining ideas as you go.

From Ideas to Actionable Plans

Generating product ideas with AI is just the beginning. In the next section, we'll explore how to refine these ideas further—optimizing features, pricing, and customer value propositions to ensure market success.

Would you like to include more real-world examples or tools, such as AI platforms ideal for product

Refining Features and Enhancing Value Propositions

Once you've generated a range of product ideas, the next step is to refine those concepts into well-defined offerings that align with customer needs. AI can play a pivotal role in optimizing product features, determining value propositions, and tailoring pricing strategies to resonate with target audiences. This process transforms raw ideas into actionable solutions primed for market success.

The Role of AI in Refinement

AI excels in refining product ideas by:

1. **Analyzing Customer Feedback:** Extracting insights from reviews, surveys, and social media to identify desirable features.

2. **Simulating Market Scenarios:** Testing hypothetical feature combinations to predict customer preferences and behavior.

3. **Benchmarking Against Competitors:** Comparing proposed features with existing market offerings to find competitive edges.

Steps to Refine Product Features Using AI

1. **Gather Data for Refinement**

   Use AI to analyze customer sentiment and preferences. Tools like natural language processing (NLP) can identify recurring themes in customer feedback.

   o **Example Prompt:**

   "Analyze customer reviews of top smartwatches and identify common complaints and desired features."

2. **Prioritize Features by Customer Value**

   Focus on features that address critical pain points or deliver unique benefits.

   o **Example Prompt:**

   "Rank the following product features based on their likely impact on customer satisfaction for a productivity app: task reminders, collaboration tools, and visual dashboards."

3. **Simulate Customer Use Cases**

   Test how proposed features work in practical scenarios using AI-driven simulations.

- o **Example Prompt:**

  "Generate use-case scenarios for a hybrid e-bike targeting urban commuters and suggest the three most valuable features for this audience."

4. **Refine Design for Accessibility and Usability**

   AI can propose adjustments to make features more user-friendly and accessible.

- o **Example Prompt:**

  "Suggest design improvements to make this fitness tracker more appealing to older adults with limited tech experience."

Crafting a Strong Value Proposition with AI

The value proposition defines why a customer would choose your product over competitors. AI can help craft compelling, customer-centric value propositions by:

1. **Highlighting Unique Benefits:** Identifying features or benefits that differentiate your product.

- o **Example Prompt:**

  "Create a value proposition for a meal-kit delivery service that emphasizes sustainability and convenience."

2. **Targeting Specific Audiences:** Tailoring messaging to appeal to different customer segments.

- o **Example Prompt:**

  "Write a value proposition for eco-conscious millennials interested in affordable reusable packaging."

3. **Simplifying Complex Concepts:** Translating technical features into clear, relatable benefits.

o **Example Prompt:**

"Rewrite this value proposition for a 5G-enabled drone delivery system in simpler terms for non-technical users."

AI-Enhanced Pricing Strategies

Pricing is a critical component of the value proposition. AI can assist by:

1. **Running Market Simulations:** Predicting customer reactions to various price points.

o **Example Prompt:**

"Based on current trends in streaming services, suggest a pricing model for a premium ad-free tier."

2. **Exploring Pricing Models:** Testing different structures such as tiered, subscription-based, or pay-as-you-go models.

o **Example Prompt:**

"Recommend pricing strategies for a new app based on a subscription model targeting small business owners."

3. **Analyzing Competitor Pricing:** Identifying pricing gaps in the market.

o **Example Prompt:**

"Compare the pricing of top fitness apps and suggest a competitive price point for a new AI-driven wellness app."

Practical Example: Refining a Health Wearable

A startup developing a health monitoring wearable used AI to refine its features. By analyzing user feedback, AI identified that customers valued longer battery life and more intuitive interfaces. Simulations suggested that offering detailed sleep analysis as a premium feature would increase perceived value. The company adjusted its product accordingly, leading to higher customer satisfaction and stronger sales.

Tips for Refinement Success

1. **Start with the Customer's Voice:** Use AI to mine customer insights and identify what matters most.

2. **Iterate Rapidly:** Use AI tools to test and refine features, value propositions, and pricing in real time.

3. **Focus on Simplicity:** Ensure that refined features enhance usability rather than complicating the product.

4. **Validate Assumptions:** Run small-scale tests to ensure that refinements align with customer needs.

Refining features and crafting a strong value proposition is a critical bridge between ideation and execution. In the next section, we'll explore how AI can help test these refined concepts, ensuring feasibility, scalability, and market fit before launching.

Optimizing Pricing and Business Models

Pricing and business models are fundamental to a product's market success. While great features and value propositions attract attention, the right pricing strategy ensures profitability and long-term sustainability. AI can help refine pricing and explore innovative business models by analyzing customer behavior, market trends, and competitor data.

The Role of AI in Pricing and Business Model Optimization

AI adds value by:

1. **Predicting Customer Sensitivity to Pricing:** Analyzing how price changes influence customer demand.

2. **Testing Various Pricing Models:** Exploring tiered, subscription-based, or pay-as-you-go options to suit diverse customer needs.

3. **Analyzing Market Trends:** Identifying pricing gaps and opportunities within a competitive landscape.

4. **Optimizing Dynamic Pricing:** Adjusting prices in real time based on demand fluctuations or seasonal trends.

Steps to Optimize Pricing with AI

1. **Assess Customer Willingness to Pay**

   AI tools can analyze purchasing patterns, survey data, and past customer behavior to estimate price tolerance.

   o **Example Prompt:**
   "Based on this customer data, suggest a pricing range for a mid-tier electric scooter targeting urban commuters."

2. **Simulate Demand Elasticity**

   Explore how changes in price affect demand for a product or service.

○ **Example Prompt:**

"Simulate the impact of a 10% price increase on demand for a premium skincare product in the U.S. market."

3. **Test Price Points Across Customer Segments**
Segment customers based on demographics, purchasing behavior, and preferences, then analyze their response to various price points.

○ **Example Prompt:**

"Analyze which pricing tier appeals most to Gen Z users of a gaming subscription service."

4. **Evaluate Competitor Pricing**
Compare your product's features and value with competitors to identify opportunities for differentiation or underpricing.

○ **Example Prompt:**

"Compare pricing structures for cloud storage services and recommend a competitive strategy for a new provider."

Exploring Business Models with AI

The right business model aligns with customer behavior and revenue goals. AI can help design, test, and refine innovative models tailored to specific markets.

Common Business Models to Explore

1. **Subscription-Based Models**: Recurring revenue through memberships or access fees.

- Example Prompt:

  "Design a subscription model for an online education platform targeting professionals seeking career advancement."

2. **Freemium Models**: Offering basic services for free and charging for premium features.

- Example Prompt:

  "Suggest freemium options for a mobile productivity app to maximize user acquisition and retention."

3. **Pay-Per-Use Models**: Charging based on the amount of product or service consumed.

- Example Prompt:

  "Create a pay-per-use model for a cloud computing service for small businesses."

4. **Dynamic Pricing Models**: Adjusting prices in real time based on demand, supply, or other variables.

- Example Prompt:

  "Develop a dynamic pricing strategy for hotel bookings during peak tourist seasons."

AI-Powered Dynamic Pricing in Action

Dynamic pricing, often used by airlines, ride-sharing platforms, and e-commerce giants, can now be tailored for smaller businesses using AI. AI can monitor market conditions, customer preferences, and competitor actions to suggest real-time pricing adjustments that maximize revenue.

- **Example Prompt:**

  "Create a dynamic pricing model for an online flower delivery service based on seasonality, inventory levels, and local competition."

Case Study: Pricing Strategy for a Meal Delivery Service

A meal delivery startup used AI to refine its pricing and business model. By analyzing customer demographics, AI identified that families were willing to pay more for subscription plans with customization options, while single customers preferred pay-per-use plans. Based on these insights, the startup introduced a hybrid pricing model: a discounted subscription plan for families and à la carte pricing for singles. This dual strategy boosted customer satisfaction and revenue.

Actionable Tips for Pricing and Business Model Optimization

1. **Emphasize Flexibility:** Test multiple pricing models before committing to one, especially in new markets.

2. **Incorporate Customer Feedback:** Use AI to monitor social media and surveys to align pricing with perceived value.

3. **Experiment with Price Anchoring:** Offer tiered pricing to guide customers toward preferred packages.

   o **Example Prompt:**

     "Suggest pricing tiers for a premium fitness app, including a basic, pro, and enterprise plan."

4. **Balance Profit and Accessibility:** Ensure pricing captures value without alienating potential customers.

Example Prompt:

"Evaluate how a 15% price cut for early adopters would impact lifetime customer value for a new wearable device."

Optimizing pricing and business models is both an art and a science, where AI acts as a powerful ally in crafting strategies grounded in data and market insights. As a next step, integrating AI to test and refine these strategies ensures alignment with real-world customer behavior and market dynamics.

Case Studies and Real-World Applications

Integrating AI into pricing strategies and business models has transformed industries by providing data-driven insights and enhancing decision-making. Below are several case studies and real-world applications demonstrating the power of AI in optimizing pricing and business models.

1. Dynamic Pricing in E-Commerce: Amazon

Challenge:
Amazon needed a way to remain competitive while maximizing profit margins across millions of products.

Solution:
Using advanced AI algorithms, Amazon implemented a dynamic pricing system that adjusts prices based on competitor pricing, demand trends, and customer behavior. AI processes massive data sets in real time, enabling price updates several times a day.

Outcome:
This system allowed Amazon to maintain competitive pricing, increase

sales volumes, and maximize profits, particularly during high-demand periods like Black Friday and Prime Day.

Key Insight:

AI can help businesses of all sizes implement dynamic pricing, ensuring competitive edge and profitability without manual intervention.

2. Personalized Pricing: Netflix

Challenge:

Netflix sought to balance customer acquisition with retention by offering pricing that reflected the value perceived by users in different regions.

Solution:

Netflix used AI to analyze data such as viewing habits, regional preferences, and economic conditions. For example, in markets with low purchasing power, the company introduced a mobile-only subscription plan at a significantly reduced price.

Outcome:

This tailored approach boosted subscriber growth in emerging markets like India and Indonesia while maintaining profitability in premium markets such as the U.S. and Europe.

Key Insight:

AI enables businesses to localize pricing and offer personalized plans that meet customer needs in diverse markets.

3. Subscription Model Refinement: Spotify

Challenge:

Spotify wanted to maximize user conversions from free to premium subscriptions while addressing customer hesitations about committing to long-term plans.

Solution:

Spotify employed AI to analyze user listening behavior and identify potential premium users. Based on these insights, it introduced targeted offers such as one-month trials and family plans to encourage upgrades.

Outcome:

The strategy resulted in higher conversion rates and reduced churn, with a significant increase in average revenue per user (ARPU).

Key Insight:

AI can identify patterns in customer behavior to craft subscription models that resonate with specific segments.

4. AI-Driven Freemium Success: Duolingo

Challenge:

Duolingo wanted to monetize its platform effectively while maintaining accessibility for free users.

Solution:

Using AI, Duolingo tracked user engagement patterns and optimized its freemium model by offering optional paid features like offline access, progress tracking, and ad removal. AI also helped analyze price sensitivity to ensure affordability across regions.

Outcome:

This approach led to significant growth in paid subscriptions, contributing to Duolingo's success as a profitable EdTech company.

Key Insight:

AI-powered freemium models can balance free value and premium monetization effectively.

5. Pay-Per-Use in Transportation: Uber

Challenge:

Uber needed a flexible pricing model to cater to varying demand across cities, times, and conditions while maximizing driver earnings and customer satisfaction.

Solution:

AI-driven algorithms adjusted fares dynamically based on factors like weather, traffic, and local demand. Uber's AI also tested multiple pricing structures for ridesharing, introducing options like UberPool to target cost-conscious customers.

Outcome:

Dynamic pricing and innovative business models enabled Uber to scale globally, attract a diverse user base, and remain competitive.

Key Insight:

Real-time AI applications in pay-per-use models can optimize pricing in volatile demand environments.

6. Predictive Pricing for Retail: Zara

Challenge:

Zara aimed to optimize pricing for new collections while minimizing unsold inventory.

Solution:

AI analyzed historical sales data, market trends, and regional preferences to set initial prices and determine when to apply discounts. It also forecasted demand for each product to adjust production and reduce waste.

Outcome:

This approach increased revenue and efficiency, enabling Zara to maintain its position as a fast-fashion leader.

Key Insight:

Predictive AI models can help balance inventory management and pricing strategies effectively.

Lessons for Practitioners

These case studies highlight several key takeaways for integrating AI into pricing and business models:

1. **Data-Driven Decisions:** AI provides clarity by processing complex data that is beyond human capability.

2. **Real-Time Adaptability:** Dynamic and responsive models enhance competitiveness.

3. **Customer-Centric Design:** Personalization fosters stronger customer relationships.

4. **Scalability:** AI allows pricing strategies to evolve with market conditions.

Actionable Insights for Readers

- **Start Small:** Test AI for pricing on a small product range or market before scaling.

- **Segment Customers:** Use AI to identify and cater to different customer groups with tailored pricing.

- **Focus on Feedback:** Continuously monitor customer responses to pricing strategies and refine accordingly.

- **Collaborate with AI Experts:** Work with data scientists to build models that align with your business goals.

Interactive Exercise: Your AI-Powered Product Idea

This hands-on activity is designed to help you practice generating and refining a product idea using AI. By following these steps, you'll experience how AI can serve as a creative partner in transforming abstract concepts into actionable insights.

Step 1: Choose a Target Market or Problem

Start by identifying a specific market or problem you want to address. Consider:

- A hobby or passion you care about.

- A frustration you've encountered in daily life.

- An emerging trend in technology, culture, or industry.

Example:
Problem: People struggle to maintain focus during remote work.

Step 2: Craft an Initial AI Prompt

Write a clear and concise prompt for your AI tool, ensuring it includes relevant details about the target market or problem. A good prompt includes:

1. **Context:** Provide background information.

2. **Goal:** What outcome are you looking for?

3. **Constraints:** Any limitations or specific criteria.

Prompt Example:

"Generate innovative product ideas to help remote workers stay focused. The solution should be low-cost, easy to implement, and compatible with existing work setups."

Step 3: Review and Refine AI Suggestions

Input your prompt into an AI tool and review the ideas it generates. Select a few promising ones and refine them by asking follow-up questions or providing additional details.

Example Output and Refinement:

- AI Idea: *A virtual assistant that monitors focus levels and provides reminders to take breaks.*

- Follow-Up Prompt: *Expand on how the virtual assistant could detect focus levels using existing technology.*

- Refined Output: *A browser extension that uses webcam-based eye-tracking and productivity timers to offer personalized focus recommendations.*

Step 4: Test Feasibility and Value

Evaluate the refined idea's feasibility, target audience, and potential value. Use AI prompts to test different aspects, such as:

- **Feasibility:** *What are the technical challenges in creating a browser extension with eye-tracking capabilities?*

- **Market Appeal:** *Who are the primary users for this tool, and what features would appeal to them most?*

- **Monetization Options:** *Suggest pricing strategies for a freemium focus-monitoring tool.*

Step 5: Create a Business Pitch Prompt

Develop a pitch using AI to summarize your idea's benefits and unique selling points.

Pitch Prompt Example:
"Draft a 100-word pitch for a browser extension that helps remote workers improve focus through AI-driven eye-tracking and productivity timers. Highlight its affordability and ease of use."

AI-Generated Pitch:
FocusSmart is the ultimate productivity tool for remote workers. This affordable browser extension uses advanced AI eye-tracking technology to monitor your focus levels, offering personalized tips to optimize your workflow. With easy integration into any setup, FocusSmart ensures you stay on track, take breaks when needed, and achieve your goals efficiently. The freemium model lets you start improving focus today, with premium options for advanced analytics. Say goodbye to distractions and hello to your most productive self with FocusSmart.

Your Turn

Now it's your time to innovate! Follow these steps:

1. Identify a problem or market you're passionate about.

2. Write your first AI prompt using the guidelines above.

3. Refine the AI's ideas and test their feasibility.

4. Create a polished pitch for your product.

   Optional Challenge: Share your product idea and pitch to gather feedback or further refine it with your team.

AI as a Catalyst for Innovation

AI has emerged as a transformative force in the innovation landscape, reshaping how individuals and organizations generate, refine, and implement ideas. By leveraging its computational power and ability to analyze vast amounts of data, AI bridges the gap between human creativity and systematic problem-solving, acting as a powerful catalyst for innovation across industries.

Redefining the Creative Process

Traditionally, innovation relied heavily on human intuition, brainstorming, and trial-and-error experimentation. While effective, these methods are often time-consuming and limited by cognitive biases and resource constraints. AI disrupts this paradigm by:

- **Expanding the Ideation Process:** AI tools can process diverse inputs, explore unconventional combinations, and suggest novel solutions that humans might overlook.

- **Accelerating Problem-Solving:** By analyzing data in real time, AI identifies patterns and insights faster than traditional methods.

- **Enhancing Collaboration:** AI fosters cross-disciplinary innovation by integrating insights from multiple fields and perspectives.

  Example: A consumer goods company used AI to develop eco-friendly packaging by analyzing global trends, customer preferences, and sustainable material options, resulting in an innovative design that boosted sales and reduced environmental impact.

How AI Drives Innovation

AI acts as a catalyst for innovation in the following ways:

1. Discovering Market Opportunities

AI can identify gaps and opportunities by analyzing customer behavior, competitor strategies, and emerging trends. Through predictive modeling and natural language processing, businesses can uncover unmet needs and anticipate future demands.

- **Example Tool:** Sentiment analysis software to evaluate customer feedback and identify pain points.

2. Generating and Refining Ideas

AI's ability to generate creative content or refine existing ideas makes it a valuable partner in brainstorming. Tools like ChatGPT can explore variations, suggest enhancements, and provide unique perspectives.

- **Example:** AI-assisted ideation platforms for product design that suggest features based on user preferences and feedback.

3. Optimizing Product and Service Design

AI enables iterative testing and refinement of products and services. By simulating user interactions and analyzing feedback, AI ensures that designs align with user expectations and market demands.

- **Example:** An AI-powered A/B testing platform helped a startup optimize its app interface, leading to a 30% increase in user retention.

4. Streamlining Prototyping and Development

AI-powered tools such as generative design software and predictive analytics expedite the prototyping process, reducing costs and time to market.

- **Example:** Automotive companies use AI to design vehicle components that maximize performance while minimizing weight and material usage.

Breaking Through Innovation Barriers

AI's capabilities are particularly effective in overcoming common barriers to innovation:

1. **Resource Constraints:** Automating repetitive tasks frees up human creativity for strategic thinking.

2. **Cognitive Biases:** AI's data-driven approach minimizes human biases, enabling objective decision-making.

3. **Fear of Risk:** AI-powered simulations allow businesses to test ideas in virtual environments before committing resources.

The Human-AI Partnership

While AI is a powerful tool, human creativity and judgment remain irreplaceable. The most successful innovations come from a synergistic partnership where AI enhances human ingenuity. By asking the right questions, defining clear goals, and iteratively collaborating with AI, innovators can achieve outcomes that surpass what either could achieve alone.

Call to Action:

Embrace AI as your co-creator. Leverage its capabilities to amplify your ideas, navigate challenges, and unlock a new era of innovation. By doing so, you position yourself and your organization at the forefront of transformative change.

Strategic Problem-Solving

Strategic problem-solving lies at the heart of decision-making in any successful organization. It's the process of dissecting challenges, analyzing potential outcomes, and identifying the most effective solutions to achieve specific goals. However, traditional approaches often fall short when dealing with complex or rapidly changing scenarios. Human biases, limited resources, and time constraints can hinder the ability to explore diverse perspectives or fully understand the nuances of a problem.

This is where AI becomes a game-changer. By leveraging its ability to process vast amounts of data, simulate scenarios, and explore problems from multiple angles, AI empowers individuals and teams to tackle challenges with unprecedented depth and efficiency. But to unlock this potential, the key lies in the art of crafting effective prompts.

AI doesn't inherently "solve" problems; instead, it responds to the questions and instructions provided by the user. The better the prompt, the more valuable the insights. Think of it as a brainstorming partner that thrives on clarity, context, and focus. With the right prompts, AI can:

- Break down complex challenges into manageable components.

- Uncover patterns, risks, and opportunities that might go unnoticed.

- Simulate outcomes and provide fresh perspectives to inform decision-making.

The Power of Strategic AI Prompts

Crafting prompts is both an art and a science. A well-structured prompt guides AI to analyze a problem comprehensively and deliver actionable insights. For instance:

- **Generic Prompt:** "Help me solve a customer service issue."

- **Strategic Prompt:** "Identify key factors causing dissatisfaction among customers in our online support system, and suggest solutions to improve response times and satisfaction rates."

Notice how the strategic prompt provides specific context and a clear objective, setting the stage for targeted insights that are immediately applicable.

AI as an Unbiased Partner

One of AI's greatest strengths is its ability to approach problems without preconceived notions or biases. While humans bring creativity, intuition, and emotional intelligence to problem-solving, we're also influenced by our experiences, beliefs, and preferences. AI complements this by offering a neutral, data-driven perspective.

For example, in a high-stakes business decision, such as whether to expand into a new market, AI can evaluate the risks and opportunities based on objective data—such as market trends, competition, and customer behavior—without being swayed by emotional attachments or office politics.

Redefining Strategic Problem-Solving

By integrating AI into strategic problem-solving, organizations and individuals can move beyond traditional brainstorming sessions and gut-feeling decisions. AI enables a more structured, informed, and innovative approach, transforming vague challenges into actionable solutions.

This section will guide readers on how to craft prompts that extract maximum value from AI, simulate diverse perspectives, and ultimately make smarter, faster, and more informed decisions. It's not just about solving problems—it's about redefining the way we approach them in an increasingly complex world.

With AI as your creative and analytical partner, strategic problem-solving becomes not only more efficient but also more innovative and impactful.

Crafting Effective Prompts for Diverse Perspectives

The key to unlocking AI's full potential for strategic problem-solving lies in how you craft your prompts. A well-crafted prompt acts as a roadmap, guiding the AI to deliver focused, insightful, and actionable responses. To analyze problems from multiple perspectives, your prompts need to be clear, specific, and structured to encourage diverse viewpoints. This section will break down the principles and techniques for crafting prompts that bring out the richness of AI's analytical capabilities.

1. Breaking Down the Problem

A good prompt starts by dissecting the challenge into its fundamental components. This helps narrow the AI's focus while covering all critical angles. Instead of asking a broad question, guide the AI toward specific aspects of the problem.

Example of a Weak Prompt:
"How do we solve supply chain issues?"

Example of a Strong Prompt:
"Identify the primary factors causing supply chain disruptions in the automotive industry, focusing on logistics, supplier relations, and global market trends. Suggest potential strategies to mitigate these challenges."

Tips for Problem Breakdown:

- Use precise language to define the problem.

- Highlight specific areas to explore, such as root causes, key stakeholders, or situational constraints.

- Incorporate relevant context to provide depth.

2. Encouraging AI to Explore Multiple Angles

AI is particularly adept at simulating various perspectives, provided the prompt explicitly asks for it. By framing the problem through different lenses, you gain insights that a singular perspective might overlook.

Techniques for Perspective Exploration:

- **Role-Based Prompts:** Ask AI to analyze the issue from the viewpoint of specific stakeholders.

  Example Prompt:

  "Examine the impact of delayed product launches from the perspectives of a customer, project manager, and investor. Suggest ways to address their unique concerns."

- **Pros vs. Cons Analysis:** Encourage the AI to weigh the advantages and disadvantages of an action or decision.

  Example Prompt:

  "What are the pros and cons of adopting a subscription-based pricing model for a software product targeting small businesses?"

- **Scenario-Based Prompts:** Explore hypothetical outcomes by asking AI to simulate "what if" scenarios.

  Example Prompt:

  "If a company switches from in-house manufacturing to outsourcing, analyze the potential impacts on cost, quality, and delivery timelines."

3. Refining Prompts Through Iteration

Rarely will the first version of a prompt yield the best results. Iteration allows you to tweak and refine prompts based on the AI's initial responses, ensuring a deeper exploration of the problem.

Steps to Refine Prompts:

1. Start with a broad prompt to identify general insights.
   Example: "What are common challenges in remote team management?"

2. Use follow-up prompts to delve into specifics.

   Follow-Up Example: "How can remote team managers maintain productivity while addressing employee burnout?"

3. Adjust parameters or clarify your request based on the AI's responses.

   Tip: If the AI's output feels generic or unfocused, add more context or constraints to guide its analysis.

4. Leveraging Comparative Prompts for Trade-Offs

Comparative prompts are particularly useful when evaluating multiple options or solutions. They help uncover trade-offs and align decisions with specific priorities.

Example Prompt:
"Compare the benefits and risks of expanding into emerging markets versus doubling down on existing markets for a mid-sized retail company."

Follow-Up Prompt:
"Focus on operational challenges, cultural differences, and growth potential in the analysis."

5. Structuring Prompts for Holistic Analysis

A holistic prompt ensures the AI considers all relevant dimensions of a problem. Structure your prompts to include:

- **Scope:** Define the context or boundaries of the problem.

- **Focus Areas:** Specify the aspects or perspectives to analyze.

- **Outcome:** Clarify what kind of insights or suggestions you're seeking.

Example of a Holistic Prompt:

"Analyze the impact of transitioning to a four-day workweek for a technology startup. Include perspectives on employee productivity, company profitability, and customer satisfaction. Provide suggestions for implementation."

6. Common Pitfalls to Avoid

When crafting prompts, be mindful of these common mistakes:

- **Vagueness:** Prompts that lack specificity will result in generic outputs.

- **Overloading the Prompt:** Asking for too many insights in one prompt can overwhelm the AI and dilute its focus.

- **Neglecting Ethical Considerations:** Avoid prompts that might inadvertently lead to biased or unethical suggestions.

Example of a Problematic Prompt:

"Suggest the cheapest way to cut costs in the workforce without considering employee satisfaction or long-term impacts."

By mastering the art of crafting prompts that encourage diverse perspectives, you can turn AI into a strategic ally capable of uncovering fresh insights, testing assumptions, and exploring solutions that go beyond conventional thinking. In the next section, we'll dive deeper into tools and techniques that further enhance AI's role in strategic problem-solving.

Tools and Techniques for Comprehensive Analysis

AI excels at conducting comprehensive analyses, provided it is guided with structured tools and techniques. By leveraging the right methods, you can ensure that the AI evaluates problems holistically, uncovers nuanced insights, and offers actionable solutions. Below are practical tools and techniques that maximize AI's analytical capabilities.

1. SWOT Analysis with AI

SWOT analysis (Strengths, Weaknesses, Opportunities, Threats) is a staple in strategic planning, and AI can enhance its depth and efficiency. By framing targeted prompts, you can have AI identify and evaluate each quadrant in the context of your problem.

Example Prompt for SWOT Analysis:
"Perform a SWOT analysis for a mid-sized e-commerce company planning to expand into international markets. Focus on operational efficiency, customer demand, regulatory challenges, and growth potential."

How AI Adds Value:

- Generates detailed lists for each quadrant, helping you uncover factors you might overlook.

- Suggests strategies to leverage strengths, address weaknesses, seize opportunities, and mitigate threats.

2. Scenario Planning with AI

Scenario planning involves exploring hypothetical situations to anticipate outcomes and prepare for uncertainties. AI can rapidly generate and analyze scenarios, providing insights into potential risks and opportunities.

Example Prompt for Scenario Planning:

"Simulate the potential outcomes if a renewable energy company shifts from a B2B to a B2C sales model. Consider impacts on revenue, operational complexity, and market perception."

Benefits of Using AI for Scenario Planning:

- Evaluates multiple "what-if" scenarios simultaneously.

- Identifies risks and mitigations across varying conditions.

- Encourages innovative approaches by suggesting unconventional strategies.

3. Root Cause Analysis

Understanding the root cause of a problem is crucial to crafting effective solutions. AI can assist by analyzing patterns, identifying systemic issues, and proposing targeted interventions.

Example Prompt for Root Cause Analysis:

"What are the root causes of declining employee engagement in a tech startup with a predominantly remote workforce? Suggest practical solutions to address these causes."

How AI Helps:

- Sifts through patterns (e.g., survey data, performance metrics) to identify underlying issues.

- Provides structured explanations and actionable recommendations.

4. Comparative Analysis

When evaluating multiple options or strategies, AI can conduct comparative analyses to highlight trade-offs, risks, and benefits. This approach is especially useful for decision-making.

Example Prompt for Comparative Analysis:

"Compare the effectiveness of launching a new product line versus expanding the existing product range for a luxury fashion brand. Focus on costs, market demand, and brand perception."

Why It's Effective:

- AI can weigh options against specific criteria, ensuring an objective evaluation.

- Highlights potential trade-offs to aid informed decision-making.

5. Data-Driven Insights and Pattern Recognition

AI thrives on processing large datasets to identify trends, correlations, and anomalies that humans might miss. By integrating data-driven prompts, you can uncover insights that form the backbone of strategic decisions.

Example Prompt for Data-Driven Insights:

"Analyze recent sales data for a SaaS company to identify seasonal trends, customer churn rates, and upsell opportunities."

Applications:

- Identifying customer segments with high potential.

- Recognizing patterns that signal risks or opportunities.

- Testing hypotheses based on historical data.

6. Decision Matrix with AI

A decision matrix helps evaluate options against a set of weighted criteria, ensuring systematic and logical decision-making. AI can simplify the process by generating or populating the matrix with relevant data.

Example Prompt for a Decision Matrix:
"Create a decision matrix to evaluate potential suppliers for a retail business. Use criteria like cost, reliability, scalability, and delivery speed."

Advantages:

- Ensures structured decision-making.

- Provides clarity by ranking options based on weighted priorities.

7. Stakeholder Analysis

Understanding the needs and concerns of stakeholders is critical in solving strategic problems. AI can help map out stakeholder dynamics and propose tailored engagement strategies.

Example Prompt for Stakeholder Analysis:
"Identify key stakeholders in a corporate restructuring plan for a manufacturing firm. Analyze their potential concerns and suggest strategies to address their interests."

Value Added by AI:

- Identifies potential conflicts or alignments among stakeholders.

- Offers communication strategies to manage expectations.

8. Multicriteria Analysis

For problems requiring evaluation across several dimensions, multicriteria analysis provides a framework for balancing competing factors. AI can assist in modeling complex scenarios and weighing priorities.

Example Prompt for Multicriteria Analysis:
"Analyze the trade-offs of opening a new production facility in either India or Mexico. Evaluate based on labor costs, market proximity, infrastructure, and regulatory environment."

Why Use AI:

- Reduces cognitive load by synthesizing large datasets.

- Balances qualitative and quantitative factors for well-rounded conclusions.

9. Simulations and Forecasting

AI can simulate outcomes based on different variables and forecast potential results. This technique is invaluable for long-term strategic planning.

Example Prompt for Forecasting:
"Forecast the potential market share of an electric vehicle company entering the Southeast Asian market in the next five years. Consider economic growth, infrastructure readiness, and consumer adoption rates."

AI's Role:

- Generates data-backed predictions.

- Highlights key variables influencing outcomes.

10. Ethical Analysis

AI can ensure that strategic decisions align with ethical principles by analyzing risks and unintended consequences.

Example Prompt for Ethical Analysis:
"Evaluate the potential ethical concerns of implementing AI-powered surveillance in public spaces. Suggest strategies to mitigate privacy risks."

How AI Contributes:

- Identifies ethical pitfalls.

- Proposes balanced approaches to address concerns.

By integrating these tools and techniques into your problem-solving processes, AI becomes more than just a helper—it evolves into a dynamic partner capable of delivering sophisticated, comprehensive analyses. The next section will showcase case studies that demonstrate the practical application of these techniques, offering a deeper understanding of how they work in real-world scenarios.

Real-World Examples of Strategic Problem-Solving with AI

To truly understand the transformative potential of AI in strategic problem-solving, it helps to explore real-world examples. These scenarios illustrate how businesses and organizations leverage AI's capabilities to address complex challenges, uncover innovative solutions, and drive actionable results.

1. Optimizing Global Supply Chains

Challenge:

A multinational retailer faced disruptions in its supply chain due to fluctuating demand, supplier delays, and geopolitical tensions. The company needed a robust strategy to predict disruptions and ensure timely deliveries.

How AI Helped:

- **Demand Forecasting:** AI analyzed historical sales data, seasonal trends, and external factors like weather and economic indicators to predict future demand with high accuracy.

- **Supplier Risk Analysis:** AI evaluated supplier performance, geopolitical risks, and transportation logistics to identify weak links in the chain.

- **Scenario Simulation:** Using AI, the company simulated various scenarios, such as port closures or raw material shortages, to assess potential impacts and prepare contingency plans.

Outcome:

The retailer reduced delivery delays by 30%, improved inventory management, and saved millions in operational costs.

2. Addressing Customer Churn in a SaaS Company

Challenge:

A SaaS provider noticed a sharp increase in customer churn, threatening its revenue growth. The team needed insights into why customers were leaving and how to retain them.

How AI Helped:

- **Churn Prediction:** AI identified patterns in user behavior, such as reduced platform usage or delayed payments, that indicated potential churn.

- **Sentiment Analysis:** By analyzing customer feedback and support tickets, AI pinpointed dissatisfaction related to specific features or service delays.

- **Personalized Interventions:** AI generated tailored retention strategies, such as offering discounts, improving onboarding processes, or prioritizing feature updates.

Outcome:

The company reduced churn by 20% in six months and increased customer satisfaction scores by focusing on targeted improvements.

3. Strategic Expansion into Emerging Markets

Challenge:

A mid-sized healthcare company aimed to expand into emerging markets but was uncertain about the risks and opportunities associated with each region.

How AI Helped:

- **Market Analysis:** AI analyzed demographic data, healthcare infrastructure, and local regulations to identify regions with the highest potential for growth.

- **Competitive Benchmarking:** By studying competitors' strategies and market share, AI highlighted opportunities for differentiation.

- **Risk Assessment:** AI identified potential challenges, such as cultural barriers, logistical constraints, and economic instability, offering tailored solutions to mitigate them.

Outcome:

The company successfully entered two new markets, achieving a 15% revenue increase in the first year.

4. Streamlining Urban Infrastructure Projects

Challenge:

A city government faced delays and cost overruns in major infrastructure projects, such as public transit expansion. They needed a way to optimize planning and execution.

How AI Helped:

- **Project Scheduling:** AI created dynamic schedules, accounting for labor availability, material procurement, and weather forecasts to minimize delays.

- **Cost Optimization:** AI identified inefficiencies in procurement and resource allocation, recommending cost-saving alternatives.

- **Community Impact Analysis:** AI simulated the social and economic impact of different project approaches, helping prioritize efforts aligned with community needs.

Outcome:

The city reduced project timelines by 20% and saved millions in unnecessary expenses while ensuring community support.

5. Improving Product Development in Consumer Tech

Challenge:

A consumer tech company was struggling to develop a new product that resonated with its target audience. Previous launches had failed due to misaligned features and pricing.

How AI Helped:

- **Consumer Insights:** AI analyzed online reviews, social media trends, and competitor offerings to understand consumer preferences and pain points.

- **Feature Prioritization:** AI evaluated which features had the highest potential for adoption based on user feedback and market research.

- **Pricing Strategy:** AI conducted simulations to test various pricing models and predicted their impact on sales and profitability.

Outcome:

The company launched a new product that became a best-seller, achieving a 25% market share within the first year.

6. Crisis Management in the Hospitality Industry

Challenge:

A global hotel chain faced a public relations crisis due to a data breach. The incident threatened customer trust and required immediate action.

How AI Helped:

- **Crisis Response Strategy:** AI analyzed similar past incidents to recommend best practices for handling the breach, including transparent communication and swift compensation offers.

- **Reputation Monitoring:** AI tracked online conversations and media coverage in real time, allowing the company to address negative sentiment proactively.

- **Future Risk Mitigation:** AI suggested enhanced cybersecurity measures and customer education initiatives to prevent future breaches.

Outcome:

The hotel chain regained customer trust and avoided significant revenue losses, with brand perception improving within three months.

7. Accelerating Drug Development in Healthcare

Challenge:

A pharmaceutical company wanted to reduce the time and cost of developing a new drug, particularly during the preclinical and clinical trial phases.

How AI Helped:

- **Compound Discovery:** AI identified promising drug compounds by analyzing vast datasets of chemical properties and previous research.

- **Clinical Trial Design:** AI simulated various trial parameters to optimize participant selection and predict trial outcomes.

- **Regulatory Insights:** AI provided recommendations for navigating complex regulatory pathways across different regions.

Outcome:

The company brought the drug to market 18 months ahead of schedule, reducing development costs by 40%.

These examples demonstrate the versatility and impact of AI in strategic problem-solving. Whether optimizing operations, exploring new opportunities, or navigating crises, AI empowers organizations to make smarter, faster, and more informed decisions. The next section will outline actionable strategies for implementing AI-driven problem-solving in your own projects and teams.

Common Pitfalls and How to Avoid Them

While AI is a powerful tool for strategic problem-solving, its effectiveness depends on how it's utilized. Missteps can lead to wasted resources, ineffective solutions, or even ethical dilemmas. This section explores some of the most common pitfalls organizations face when using AI for problem-solving and actionable strategies to overcome them.

1. Poorly Defined Problems

The Pitfall:
AI tools are only as effective as the clarity of the problems they aim to solve. Vague or overly broad problem definitions often result in generic, unhelpful outputs.

How to Avoid It:

- Clearly articulate the problem with specific goals and constraints.

- Use targeted prompts that include the context, desired outcomes, and key variables.

- Collaborate with stakeholders to ensure the problem is well understood from multiple perspectives before involving AI.

Example:

Instead of asking AI to "reduce costs," refine the prompt to "identify opportunities to reduce operational costs by 10% within our logistics department without impacting delivery times."

2. Over-Reliance on AI

The Pitfall:

Some organizations delegate too much responsibility to AI, expecting it to solve problems independently without human oversight. This can lead to flawed solutions, as AI lacks intuition, emotional intelligence, and ethical reasoning.

How to Avoid It:

- Treat AI as a co-pilot rather than the sole decision-maker.

- Validate AI-generated insights with human expertise and domain knowledge.

- Foster a culture that blends AI's computational power with human creativity and critical thinking.

Example:

A marketing team might use AI to generate campaign ideas but should still rely on human insights to ensure the messaging aligns with brand values and audience expectations.

3. Ignoring Data Quality

The Pitfall:

AI relies on data to generate insights. If the input data is incomplete, outdated, or biased, the outputs will reflect these flaws, leading to inaccurate or skewed results.

How to Avoid It:

- Regularly audit and clean your data to ensure it's relevant and reliable.

- Diversify datasets to reduce biases and improve the robustness of AI outputs.

- Use synthetic data or simulations to fill gaps in datasets where real-world data is unavailable.

Example:
A hiring platform that trains AI on biased historical hiring data risks perpetuating discriminatory practices. Addressing this requires careful data preprocessing and bias testing.

4. Failing to Interpret Results Critically

The Pitfall:
AI outputs can seem definitive, but they are often probabilistic and should not be taken at face value without deeper analysis. Blindly following AI-generated recommendations can lead to misinformed decisions.

How to Avoid It:

- Examine the logic or patterns behind AI recommendations.

- Use AI to present multiple solutions and compare their potential impacts.

- Encourage teams to question and refine AI outputs before implementing them.

Example:

If AI suggests cutting costs by reducing employee benefits, consider the long-term implications for morale, productivity, and turnover rates before proceeding.

5. Neglecting Ethical Considerations

The Pitfall:

Using AI without considering its ethical implications can result in privacy violations, algorithmic bias, or unintended harm to stakeholders.

How to Avoid It:

- Prioritize transparency in how AI decisions are made.

- Test algorithms for bias and adjust them as needed.

- Ensure compliance with legal and ethical standards, particularly in sensitive industries like healthcare and finance.

Example:

An AI-driven lending platform should regularly test its algorithms to ensure that applicants from all demographics are treated fairly and equitably.

6. Unrealistic Expectations

The Pitfall:

Believing that AI can solve all problems instantly can lead to frustration and disillusionment when results fall short of expectations.

How to Avoid It:

- Set realistic goals for what AI can achieve within specific timelines.

- Recognize that AI is most effective when used as part of a broader strategy.

- Start with smaller, manageable projects to build confidence and understanding before scaling up.

Example:
Instead of expecting AI to revolutionize an entire organization overnight, focus on using it to optimize one process, such as inventory management, before expanding its role.

7. Inadequate Training and Adoption

The Pitfall:
Teams may resist or misuse AI tools due to a lack of understanding or training, limiting their potential impact.

How to Avoid It:

- Provide comprehensive training on how to use AI effectively, including crafting prompts and interpreting results.

- Involve teams early in the process to foster buy-in and address concerns.

- Highlight success stories to demonstrate AI's value.

Example:
A company introducing AI for customer service might organize workshops to train agents on using AI chatbots, ensuring they complement human interactions rather than replacing them.

8. Overlooking Long-Term Implications

The Pitfall:

Short-term solutions generated by AI might have unintended long-term consequences, such as unsustainable practices or reputational risks.

How to Avoid It:

- Use AI to explore not just immediate solutions but also their future impacts through scenario simulations.

- Regularly revisit strategies to ensure they remain relevant and beneficial over time.

Example:

A company using AI to optimize packaging costs might discover later that the chosen materials harm its sustainability commitments. Addressing such issues upfront can prevent conflicts with corporate values.

By understanding and addressing these common pitfalls, organizations can harness AI as a truly effective partner in strategic problem-solving. Success lies in balancing the technology's capabilities with human oversight, critical thinking, and ethical responsibility. This ensures that AI delivers meaningful, sustainable, and impactful solutions.

Actionable Takeaways and Prompt Templates

This section provides readers with actionable steps to integrate AI into their strategic problem-solving processes effectively. Additionally, it includes prompt templates that readers can use and adapt for various problem-solving scenarios.

Actionable Takeaways

1. **Start with a Clear Problem Statement:**

o   Ensure your problem is well-defined and specific, including constraints, goals, and context. Ambiguity leads to suboptimal AI outputs.

2. **Leverage AI to Explore Multiple Perspectives:**

o   Craft prompts that ask AI to analyze problems from diverse angles, industries, or stakeholder viewpoints. This broadens the scope of potential solutions.

3. **Combine AI with Human Expertise:**

o   Use AI to generate ideas, then refine them using human judgment, creativity, and contextual understanding.

4. **Iterate on Prompts for Better Outputs:**

o   Experiment with different prompt structures to guide the AI toward more useful insights. Be iterative—refine, adjust, and test.

5. **Simulate Scenarios for Long-Term Thinking:**

o   Use AI to model the potential outcomes of various solutions, considering both short-term results and long-term implications.

6. **Integrate Ethical Considerations:**

o   Ask AI to identify possible ethical or social impacts of a proposed solution and suggest ways to mitigate risks.

7. **Evaluate Feasibility and Scalability:**

o   Use AI to assess whether proposed ideas are practical, cost-effective, and scalable across different contexts.

Prompt Templates

Here are some ready-to-use prompt templates tailored to different aspects of strategic problem-solving.

1. Understanding the Problem:

"Analyze [specific problem] in the context of [industry or organization]. Identify the root causes, key contributing factors, and potential risks associated with this issue."
Example:
"Analyze declining customer retention rates in the context of a subscription-based software company. Identify root causes, key contributing factors, and risks."

2. Generating Multiple Perspectives:

"How might [specific problem] be viewed or addressed from the perspective of [stakeholder/discipline]? Provide at least three unique approaches or viewpoints."
Example:
"How might supply chain delays be viewed or addressed from the perspective of logistics managers, suppliers, and end consumers? Provide at least three unique approaches."

3. Prioritizing Solutions:

"Given [list of possible solutions], rank them based on [criteria such as cost, feasibility, or impact]. Provide a brief justification for each ranking."
Example:
"Given three possible solutions for reducing employee turnover—offering higher salaries, flexible work hours, or additional training opportunities—rank them based on cost, feasibility, and impact. Provide a brief justification for each ranking."

4. Simulating Scenarios:

"If [specific solution] is implemented, predict the potential outcomes over [time period]. Highlight short-term benefits, long-term challenges, and any risks or uncertainties."
Example:

"If the company adopts a remote-first work policy, predict the potential outcomes over the next two years. Highlight short-term benefits, long-term challenges, and risks."

5. Addressing Ethical Implications:

"What ethical or social considerations should be accounted for when implementing [specific solution]? Suggest ways to mitigate potential risks."

Example:

"What ethical or social considerations should be accounted for when using AI to automate customer service? Suggest ways to mitigate potential risks."

6. Enhancing Collaboration:

"Suggest ways to align diverse perspectives and priorities among [stakeholders/teams] to address [specific problem]."

Example:

"Suggest ways to align diverse perspectives and priorities among the marketing, sales, and product teams to address declining user engagement."

7. Testing Feasibility and Scalability:

"Evaluate the feasibility and scalability of [specific solution] for [specific context or market]. Identify potential obstacles and suggest improvements."

Example:

"Evaluate the feasibility and scalability of using renewable energy sources for a mid-sized manufacturing company. Identify potential obstacles and suggest improvements."

8. Crafting Long-Term Strategies:

"Develop a long-term strategy to address [specific problem], considering trends, risks, and opportunities over the next [time period]."

Example:

"Develop a long-term strategy to address talent shortages in the healthcare industry, considering trends, risks, and opportunities over the next decade."

These takeaways and prompt templates equip readers with practical tools to navigate the complexities of strategic problem-solving using AI. By combining well-crafted prompts with critical human oversight, organizations can unlock new levels of insight and innovation.

Marketing and Campaign Ideation

Modern marketing operates in an environment of unprecedented complexity. The sheer volume of advertisements, campaigns, and content produced daily creates a fierce battle for consumer attention. Companies face mounting pressure to differentiate themselves and capture the imagination of increasingly discerning audiences. Yet, in this pursuit, marketers often encounter significant challenges—creative blocks, data overload, and rapidly shifting consumer expectations, among others.

The marketing landscape demands agility, creativity, and data-driven strategies. Traditional brainstorming methods, while valuable, often fall short in addressing the fast-paced, multidimensional demands of today's campaigns. Teams may struggle with groupthink, rely too heavily on past strategies, or fail to account for the diversity of modern audiences. These limitations call for innovative tools and approaches to maintain relevance and impact.

The Complexity of Modern Marketing

Marketing today is no longer a one-size-fits-all endeavor. The rise of digital platforms has fragmented audiences into micro-segments, each with unique preferences, behaviors, and cultural contexts. A campaign that resonates with one demographic may alienate another. Furthermore, the proliferation of social media means that brand messaging must be adaptable, concise, and engaging across multiple platforms.

Consider a global brand launching a new product. The campaign must be culturally sensitive, visually appealing, and compelling enough to stand out in a consumer's social media feed. It must also align with the brand's overall identity while addressing local market nuances. Achieving this balance requires deep insights, creativity, and efficient collaboration—demands that traditional brainstorming struggles to meet consistently.

Adding to the challenge is the increasing demand for personalized marketing. Consumers now expect tailored experiences, from ads that reflect their interests to emails that address their specific needs. This personalization requires not only data analysis but also innovative ideas that can connect emotionally with different audiences. Traditional methods often lack the tools to effectively translate data into creative solutions, creating a gap that hinders marketing success.

The Limits of Traditional Brainstorming

Despite its ubiquity, traditional brainstorming is fraught with challenges in marketing contexts. Teams often encounter creative ruts, relying on familiar ideas rather than exploring fresh perspectives. Group dynamics, such as dominant voices or conformity pressure, can stifle innovation. Moreover, brainstorming sessions are frequently time-intensive, requiring significant coordination and resources with no guarantee of actionable outcomes.

A significant drawback of traditional brainstorming is its difficulty in integrating data-driven insights. While marketers may have access to rich data on consumer preferences, campaign performance, and market trends, translating this information into creative concepts often proves elusive. Data analysis tools and marketing intuition may exist in silos, preventing a seamless flow of information into the ideation process.

Furthermore, the reliance on human creativity alone introduces inherent biases. Personal experiences, cultural norms, and subconscious assumptions shape the ideas generated, limiting the scope of solutions. For instance, a team brainstorming ideas for a product targeting Gen Z may unintentionally apply millennial-focused perspectives, resulting in messaging that misses the mark.

The Need for Speed and Scale

In the digital age, time is a critical factor in marketing success. Trends emerge and fade rapidly, requiring brands to act quickly to capitalize on opportunities. Traditional brainstorming, with its iterative and often slow-paced nature, struggles to keep up with the urgency of modern campaigns. Teams may find themselves under pressure to generate ideas within tight deadlines, leading to rushed or suboptimal outcomes.

Additionally, marketing at scale demands an ability to produce diverse, high-quality content that caters to various platforms and audiences. A single campaign may require video scripts, social media posts, email newsletters, and ad copy—all tailored to different segments. Meeting this demand manually is resource-intensive and often results in inconsistent quality.

These challenges highlight the limitations of traditional approaches to ideation in marketing. They also underscore the need for tools that can streamline the creative process, enhance collaboration, and enable rapid iteration without sacrificing quality.

The Promise of AI in Marketing

This is where Artificial Intelligence (AI) enters the equation. AI has the potential to address many of the challenges marketers face by serving as a tireless, unbiased, and highly adaptable brainstorming partner. Unlike traditional brainstorming, AI can process vast amounts of data in seconds, identify emerging trends, and generate diverse ideas tailored to specific needs.

By leveraging AI, marketers can move beyond the bottlenecks of traditional methods. They can explore a broader range of possibilities, adapt quickly to market shifts, and produce creative solutions at scale. The key to unlocking this potential lies in **prompt engineering**, the skill of crafting precise inputs that guide AI systems to deliver actionable insights.

In the next section, we'll delve deeper into how AI changes the game for marketing ideation, exploring its capabilities and the transformative impact it can have on creativity and strategy.

Unleashing Creativity with AI

Creativity is the lifeblood of successful advertising campaigns, and the ability to craft original and engaging ad concepts can make or break a brand's connection with its audience. However, even the most talented marketing teams face creative blocks and fatigue. This is where AI steps in, acting as an innovative brainstorming partner capable of generating fresh ideas at scale. Unlike humans, AI doesn't tire, is free of biases, and has the capability to draw inspiration from diverse fields, historical campaigns, and vast datasets in seconds.

AI's ability to analyze patterns and trends across industries allows it to suggest concepts that are both imaginative and data-informed. For example, an AI system could analyze the visual styles of high-performing campaigns in the fashion industry and suggest concepts that merge popular elements with emerging cultural themes. This dynamic combination of creativity and data-driven insight makes AI a revolutionary tool in ad ideation.

Prompt Engineering for Ad Concept Generation

The magic of AI in advertising lies in its ability to respond to well-crafted prompts. Prompt engineering is the key to unlocking AI's creative potential, ensuring the ideas it generates align with a brand's goals, values, and target audience. A generic prompt such as "Create an ad for a smartphone" might yield broad, uninspired results. However, a specific and detailed prompt like "Generate five ad concepts for a smartphone targeting tech-savvy millennials, emphasizing sustainability and innovative design" provides the AI with the guidance needed to produce relevant, high-quality ideas.

Marketers can refine their prompts by including additional context, such as the intended tone, desired emotional response, or unique selling points of the product. For example:

- **Basic Prompt**: "Create an ad for a health drink."

- **Enhanced Prompt**: "Generate three ad concepts for a health drink targeting young professionals, highlighting its immunity-boosting benefits and eco-friendly packaging. Use an optimistic tone and appeal to an active lifestyle."

The iterative nature of AI also allows marketers to refine their results by tweaking prompts or combining ideas from multiple outputs. This process ensures that the final concepts are not only creative but also strategically aligned with the campaign objectives.

Case Study: Eco-Friendly Water Bottles

Let's consider a fictional product: a reusable, eco-friendly water bottle designed for outdoor enthusiasts. A marketing team might use AI to brainstorm ad concepts with the following prompt: "Create five ad concepts for a reusable, eco-friendly water bottle targeting environmentally conscious hikers and campers. Highlight the product's durability, design, and impact on reducing plastic waste."

AI-generated responses might include:

1. **Concept 1**: A visual of a rugged mountain landscape with the tagline, "Your adventure, without the waste." The ad emphasizes durability and environmental benefits, with a hiker holding the water bottle against the backdrop of a pristine, trash-free trail.

2. **Concept 2**: A split-screen ad comparing a pile of disposable plastic bottles to a single eco-friendly bottle, with the tagline, "One choice, endless adventures."

3. **Concept 3**: A social media campaign inviting users to share their hiking stories with the bottle using the hashtag #EcoTrailTales.

4. **Concept 4**: A humorous video ad showing a bottle "rescuing" a hiker from carrying heavy disposable bottles, ending with the slogan, "Pack lighter, live greener."

5. **Concept 5**: An interactive online ad featuring a calculator that shows users how many disposable bottles they can replace by switching to the product.

Each concept is tailored to resonate with the target audience's values and lifestyle, showcasing the product's benefits in a compelling and creative way.

Cross-Industry Inspiration

One of the most valuable features of AI in ad ideation is its ability to pull inspiration from unrelated industries. For instance, an AI system might analyze storytelling techniques from movie trailers, visual aesthetics from art galleries, or engagement strategies from gaming apps. These insights can lead to unexpected and innovative ad concepts that break traditional molds.

For example, an AI brainstorming session for a new line of sneakers might draw on the suspense-building techniques used in thriller films, suggesting an ad concept that teases the "hidden power" of the sneakers before revealing their performance-enhancing features. This interdisciplinary approach helps brands stay ahead of the curve and create campaigns that stand out in a saturated market.

Practical Tools and Techniques

To maximize the impact of AI in ad ideation, marketers should use platforms and tools designed for creative brainstorming. Many AI tools offer features such as:

- **Mood and Tone Customization**: Allowing users to specify whether the ad should be humorous, inspirational, or sentimental.

- **Visual Style Recommendations**: Generating ideas for color schemes, imagery, and layouts based on brand identity.

- **Market Trend Integration**: Suggesting concepts that align with current cultural or industry trends.

By combining these tools with prompt engineering expertise, marketers can not only generate creative ad concepts but also refine and adapt them to fit diverse campaign goals.

The Creative Edge

AI has transformed the way marketers approach ad concept generation. By combining boundless creativity with data-driven precision, it offers solutions to many of the challenges that traditional brainstorming methods fail to address. With the power of prompt engineering, marketers can harness AI to produce engaging, relevant, and innovative campaigns that resonate with their audiences.

In the next section, we will explore the art of crafting memorable taglines that stick, delving deeper into how AI can help capture the essence of a brand in just a few words.

The Importance of a Memorable Tagline

A tagline is more than just a catchy phrase—it's a brand's calling card. The right tagline distills the essence of a company's identity, values, and promises into a few words that resonate emotionally and remain in the minds of consumers long after they encounter it. Think of Nike's "Just Do It" or Apple's "Think Different." These taglines encapsulate entire brand philosophies while inspiring action and loyalty.

However, crafting a tagline that sticks is no simple feat. It requires a deep understanding of the brand, its target audience, and the cultural context in which the brand operates. The challenge is magnified in today's crowded digital marketplace, where brands vie for attention in an environment saturated with noise. A successful tagline must cut through this noise, creating an immediate connection with its audience while maintaining relevance over time.

AI's Role in Tagline Generation

AI brings a new dimension to tagline creation by combining its ability to process vast amounts of data with the creative potential unlocked by well-engineered prompts. While human creativity often involves iterative trial and error, AI can generate hundreds of tagline variations in seconds, offering marketers a broad range of options to evaluate and refine.

AI is particularly effective in analyzing market trends, consumer behavior, and competitive positioning to inform tagline creation. For instance, an AI system can study high-performing taglines in a specific industry, identify common linguistic patterns or themes, and use that information to suggest new taglines tailored to a brand's unique value proposition. This process ensures that the tagline is both innovative and rooted in data-driven insights.

Prompt Engineering for Taglines

The quality of AI-generated taglines depends largely on the prompts provided. Effective prompts are specific, contextual, and aligned with the brand's goals. A vague prompt like "Generate taglines for a coffee brand" may produce uninspired results, whereas a detailed prompt such as "Suggest five taglines for a premium coffee brand that emphasizes sustainability, fair trade, and artisanal quality. The tone should be sophisticated yet approachable" will yield more relevant and creative outputs.

Here are examples of prompts for various industries:

- **Fitness App**: "Generate three taglines for a fitness app targeting busy professionals, highlighting convenience, personalization, and results."

- **Electric Vehicle**: "Create five taglines for a new electric vehicle brand that appeals to environmentally conscious urban millennials. Emphasize innovation and sustainability."

- **Luxury Watch**: "Suggest three taglines for a luxury watch brand that embodies timeless elegance and craftsmanship."

AI thrives on iteration, allowing marketers to refine prompts and experiment with different angles. For instance, if the initial tagline suggestions lack emotional impact, the prompt can be adjusted to emphasize inspiration or urgency.

Real-World Examples of AI-Generated Taglines

To illustrate how AI can assist in tagline creation, let's consider a fictional eco-friendly home cleaning brand called "Green Spark." A detailed prompt might be: "Generate five taglines for an eco-friendly home cleaning product line called 'Green Spark.' Focus on sustainability, effectiveness, and creating a healthier home environment. The tone should be modern and uplifting."

AI-generated suggestions could include:

1. "Green Spark: Clean Home, Clean Planet."

2. "Powerful Cleaning, Naturally."

3. "Eco-Friendly Solutions for Everyday Messes."

4. "Sparkling Clean, Sustainably Done."

5. "Green Spark: Because Your Home Deserves Better."

Each tagline reflects the brand's values while appealing to its environmentally conscious target audience. The marketer can then evaluate these options, refine them further, or combine elements to create the perfect tagline.

Balancing Creativity and Strategy

While AI can provide countless tagline ideas, human oversight is essential to ensure the final choice aligns with the brand's identity and strategic goals. A tagline must not only be memorable but also authentic, adaptable, and legally viable. For example, AI may generate a tagline that is compelling but too similar to an existing tagline from a competitor, posing potential legal and branding risks.

Marketers can use AI to streamline the ideation process and test different tagline options across focus groups or online surveys. AI can also analyze consumer responses to different taglines, providing insights into which phrases resonate most with the target audience.

Iterative Tagline Refinement

The iterative nature of AI-powered brainstorming allows marketers to explore multiple directions for a tagline. Here's a practical example of how prompts can evolve during the refinement process:

1. **Initial Prompt**: "Suggest taglines for a sustainable skincare brand."

o Output: "Glow Naturally," "Sustain Your Beauty," "Eco-Friendly Radiance."

2. **Refined Prompt**: "Focus on self-care and environmental impact."

o Output: "Nurture Yourself, Protect the Planet," "Beauty Meets Sustainability," "Kind to You, Kind to Earth."

3. **Final Prompt**: "Add a luxurious and sophisticated tone."

o Output: "Sustainable Elegance for Your Skin," "Where Nature Meets Refinement," "Elevated Care, Naturally."

By iterating, marketers can arrive at a tagline that balances emotional resonance, brand values, and audience appeal.

The Emotional Impact of a Tagline

A great tagline doesn't just convey information—it evokes emotion. Whether it inspires trust, joy, ambition, or nostalgia, the emotional impact of a tagline is what makes it memorable. AI can assist in crafting taglines that tap into specific emotions by analyzing the language and tone that resonate with target demographics. For instance, AI can use sentiment analysis to suggest words and phrases that evoke positivity, urgency, or aspiration.

Conclusion: Crafting Taglines That Endure

Taglines are a cornerstone of brand identity, encapsulating what a company stands for in just a few words. With the help of AI and prompt engineering, marketers can unlock new levels of creativity and precision in tagline creation. By combining AI's ability to generate diverse ideas with human intuition and strategy, brands can craft taglines that stick—leaving a lasting impression on audiences and standing the test of time.

The Importance of Cohesion in Branding

A cohesive branding strategy is the backbone of a strong and memorable brand. It ensures that every touchpoint—whether a social media post, a product package, or an ad campaign—consistently conveys the brand's identity, values, and promises. Cohesion builds trust, reinforces recognition, and creates emotional connections with consumers.

In today's fragmented digital landscape, maintaining a unified brand presence is more challenging than ever. Brands operate across multiple channels, cater to diverse audiences, and face constant pressure to adapt to emerging trends. Without a cohesive strategy, these efforts can feel disjointed and dilute the brand's impact. AI, with its ability to synthesize data, analyze trends, and generate creative content, offers marketers an unprecedented opportunity to build and maintain cohesive branding strategies efficiently and effectively.

Challenges in Building Cohesive Branding Strategies

Developing and executing a unified branding strategy requires navigating several challenges, including:

1. **Inconsistent Messaging**: Different teams or agencies managing marketing efforts may interpret brand guidelines differently, leading to variations in tone, language, or visual style.

2. **Multi-Channel Complexity**: Maintaining consistency across platforms with different formats and audience expectations—such as Instagram, LinkedIn, email newsletters, and physical packaging—can be daunting.

3. **Audience Segmentation**: Catering to diverse demographic or geographic segments often leads to mixed messaging, making it hard to maintain a singular brand voice.

4. **Evolving Trends**: Adapting to cultural shifts and technological advances while staying true to a brand's identity is a delicate balancing act.

These challenges underscore the need for tools that can help streamline the process, ensure alignment, and provide creative flexibility without compromising brand integrity.

How AI Reinforces Brand Cohesion

AI plays a transformative role in creating cohesive branding strategies. By integrating data analysis, automation, and creative ideation, AI helps marketers align every aspect of a brand's presence, ensuring that messaging, visuals, and tone remain consistent across all channels.

1. **Centralizing Brand Guidelines**: AI tools can store and manage detailed brand guidelines, making them easily accessible to all teams and ensuring consistency in tone, style, and visual elements. For example, AI can recommend approved color schemes, fonts, and tone of voice when generating content.

2. **Multi-Channel Optimization**: AI's ability to adapt content to different platforms ensures that campaigns are tailored to fit the unique requirements of each channel while maintaining a unified voice. For instance, the same message can be formatted as a short tweet, a detailed LinkedIn post, and an engaging Instagram reel.

3. **Real-Time Monitoring**: AI can analyze live campaigns to detect inconsistencies in branding, offering real-time feedback to ensure alignment. This capability allows marketers to course-correct quickly and avoid potential branding mishaps.

4. **Personalization Without Fragmentation**: AI enables brands to personalize content for specific audiences while maintaining overall cohesion. By analyzing audience data, AI can suggest variations of a core message that resonate with different demographics while staying true to the brand identity.

The Role of Prompt Engineering in Branding Strategy

Prompt engineering is critical to harnessing AI effectively for cohesive branding. The quality of the prompts determines how well the AI understands and aligns with the brand's identity. For example:

- **Basic Prompt**: "Generate content for a skincare brand."

- **Detailed Prompt**: "Create a social media post for a luxury skincare brand that targets eco-conscious millennials. The tone should be sophisticated yet approachable, and the visuals should emphasize natural ingredients and minimalism."

The latter prompt ensures that AI-generated content aligns with the brand's image, audience, and values. Marketers can refine prompts further to address specific needs, such as creating content for a particular platform or tailoring messaging for a regional audience.

Case Study: AI in Branding for a Global Fitness Brand

Imagine a global fitness brand aiming to launch a new campaign promoting inclusivity and empowerment. The brand's challenge is to maintain a unified voice while addressing diverse cultural contexts and consumer preferences.

Using AI, the brand could achieve the following:

1. **Unified Messaging**: The brand develops a core slogan, such as "Strength in Every Step," and uses AI to generate platform-specific variations. For instance, a TikTok caption might read, "Your strength inspires us all 💪 #StrengthInEveryStep," while an email campaign might say, "Discover the strength that moves you forward."

2. **Visual Consistency**: AI recommends imagery, color palettes, and graphic styles that align with the brand's guidelines, ensuring all campaign materials look and feel cohesive.

3. **Localized Adaptation**: AI helps the brand adapt its messaging for different regions, ensuring cultural sensitivity without straying from the core message. For example, in regions where group fitness is popular, AI might suggest imagery and copy emphasizing community workouts, while in areas where solo training is preferred, the focus might shift to individual empowerment.

4. **Campaign Analysis**: Throughout the campaign, AI monitors audience engagement and sentiment across platforms, identifying opportunities to optimize content while maintaining alignment with the brand's strategy.

Building Brand Narratives with AI

Cohesive branding is about more than just consistent messaging—it's about telling a compelling story that resonates across all touchpoints. AI can assist in building brand narratives by identifying common themes in consumer feedback, analyzing competitor campaigns, and generating story-driven content ideas. For instance, an AI system might suggest a video series highlighting customer success stories or a social media campaign celebrating the brand's impact on local communities.

By integrating these elements into the broader branding strategy, marketers can create a narrative that feels authentic, relatable, and memorable.

Conclusion: AI as a Branding Ally

Building a cohesive branding strategy is essential for creating a strong and lasting impression in today's competitive marketplace. AI empowers marketers to overcome traditional challenges by streamlining processes, enhancing creativity, and ensuring consistency across channels and audiences.

By leveraging prompt engineering and AI-driven insights, brands can craft strategies that not only align with their core identity but also adapt to the ever-changing demands of the modern consumer. With AI as a branding ally, marketers can deliver campaigns that are as cohesive as they are impactful, creating a unified voice that resonates in every corner of the market.

In the next section, we'll explore **strategies for tailoring messaging to different audiences,** diving deeper into how AI enables brands to balance personalization with brand integrity.

The Need for Personalized Messaging

In today's diverse and highly segmented marketplace, one-size-fits-all messaging no longer works. Audiences vary in their values, preferences, cultural contexts, and buying behaviors. To connect effectively, brands must tailor their messaging to resonate with different groups while maintaining the essence of their identity.

This challenge is amplified by the increasing number of communication channels, each with its own unique audience demographics and content demands. Tailored messaging is no longer just about altering tone or phrasing—it's about understanding the audience's needs, motivations, and pain points and addressing them in a way that feels personal, relevant, and authentic.

AI has become a powerful tool for achieving this level of personalization at scale. By analyzing data, identifying patterns, and crafting contextually relevant content, AI allows brands to deliver the right message to the right audience at the right time, without losing cohesion in their overall branding strategy.

The Role of Audience Segmentation

Audience segmentation is the cornerstone of tailored messaging. Traditionally, marketers have segmented audiences based on demographics such as age, gender, income, and location. However, modern segmentation goes deeper, incorporating psychographics (e.g., values, lifestyle, interests), behavioral data (e.g., purchase history, online activity), and even emotional triggers.

AI enhances this process by analyzing massive datasets to identify patterns and insights that humans might miss. For example, AI can segment an audience into micro-groups based on subtle preferences, such as:

- Frequent buyers versus occasional shoppers.

- Consumers who prioritize eco-friendliness over affordability.

- Social media users who engage with humorous content versus those who prefer educational posts.

With these nuanced segments, brands can craft messages that speak directly to the unique motivations and preferences of each group, increasing the likelihood of engagement and conversion.

AI in Tailoring Messaging

AI excels at tailoring messaging through its ability to process and generate content based on detailed inputs. Here's how it works across different aspects of marketing:

1. **Analyzing Audience Data**: AI tools analyze social media activity, search behavior, and purchasing patterns to create detailed audience profiles. For example, an AI system might determine that one segment values luxury and exclusivity, while another prioritizes affordability and practicality.

2. **Adapting Tone and Style**: AI can adjust the tone, style, and vocabulary of content to align with the preferences of each audience segment. For instance, messaging for Gen Z might use playful language and emojis, while messaging for C-suite executives would adopt a more formal, data-driven tone.

3. **Contextual Content Creation**: Using prompt engineering, marketers can guide AI to generate content tailored to specific audiences. A prompt like, "Create a social media post for a health-conscious millennial audience promoting plant-based protein shakes. Emphasize taste and sustainability with a casual tone," ensures relevance and resonance.

4. **Localization and Cultural Sensitivity**: AI helps brands adapt their messaging for different regions, languages, and cultural contexts. For example, AI can ensure that marketing copy for an international audience avoids idioms or cultural references that might not translate well.

Crafting Tailored Prompts for Audience Messaging

The effectiveness of AI in tailoring messaging depends on the quality of the prompts provided. A vague prompt may yield generic results, while a well-crafted one ensures content is aligned with the target audience's needs and preferences.

Here are examples of tailored prompts for different audience segments:

- **High-Income Consumers**:
  Prompt: "Generate ad copy for a luxury watch brand targeting affluent professionals. The tone should be sophisticated and aspirational, emphasizing exclusivity and craftsmanship."

- **Eco-Conscious Millennials**:
  Prompt: "Write a social media post for an eco-friendly home cleaning product. The tone should be modern and casual, highlighting sustainability and the health benefits of natural ingredients."

- **Parents of Young Children**:
  Prompt: "Create a blog headline for a brand of organic baby food that reassures parents about nutrition and safety. Emphasize trust and family values."

- **Tech Enthusiasts**:
  Prompt: "Generate a promotional email for a new smart home device targeting tech-savvy individuals. Highlight innovation, convenience, and compatibility with existing devices."

By experimenting with and refining prompts, marketers can achieve hyper-targeted messaging that resonates deeply with each audience segment.

Real-World Example: Tailored Messaging in Action

Consider a fitness apparel brand launching a new line of sustainable activewear. Using AI, the brand could create tailored messaging for different audience segments:

1. **Athletes and Fitness Enthusiasts**:

- Message: "Gear up for peak performance with sustainable activewear engineered for ultimate comfort and durability."

- Channel: Fitness blogs, sports-focused Instagram pages.

2. **Eco-Conscious Shoppers**:

- Message: "Choose activewear that respects the planet—made from recycled materials and designed to last."

- Channel: Sustainability forums, eco-friendly shopping apps.

3. **Casual Buyers**:

- Message: "Look good, feel great—activewear that combines style, comfort, and sustainability."

- Channel: Lifestyle influencers, online fashion stores.

4. **Discount Seekers**:

- Message: "Affordable style, uncompromised quality—get 20% off our sustainable activewear collection today!"

- Channel: Email newsletters, discount websites.

    By tailoring messaging to each group, the brand can maximize engagement and drive conversions while reinforcing its identity as a sustainable and inclusive company.

Balancing Personalization and Brand Cohesion

While tailored messaging is essential, it's equally important to maintain a cohesive brand identity. This means ensuring that all messages, regardless of the audience segment, reflect the brand's core values, tone, and visual style. AI aids in this by centralizing brand guidelines and applying them consistently across all content.

For example, while the tone might vary—playful for Gen Z and formal for business professionals—the underlying themes of quality and trust should remain constant. AI tools can flag inconsistencies and suggest adjustments to ensure alignment with the brand's overall strategy.

Measuring the Impact of Tailored Messaging

AI also plays a key role in measuring the success of tailored messaging. By analyzing engagement metrics, conversion rates, and customer feedback, AI provides insights into what works and what doesn't. This data allows marketers to refine their messaging further, creating a continuous cycle of improvement.

For example, if an AI system detects that eco-conscious shoppers respond more positively to messaging that emphasizes carbon footprint reduction over recycled materials, the brand can adjust its strategy accordingly.

Conclusion: The Future of Personalized Messaging

Tailoring messaging to different audiences is no longer optional—it's a necessity for brands looking to build meaningful connections and drive results. With AI and prompt engineering, marketers can achieve unprecedented levels of personalization, delivering content that resonates with diverse audiences while maintaining a unified brand presence.

The Fast-Paced World of Modern Marketing

In today's hypercompetitive marketplace, speed is everything. Campaigns must be developed, tested, and launched in record time to stay ahead of trends and respond to shifting consumer preferences. Traditional campaign development, with its reliance on brainstorming sessions, iterative design processes, and multi-layered approvals, often falls short in meeting these demands.

AI has emerged as a game-changer, enabling marketers to streamline campaign development while maintaining creativity and quality. By automating repetitive tasks, generating fresh ideas, and offering data-driven insights, AI empowers teams to deliver impactful campaigns at a fraction of the time and cost. In this chapter, we explore how AI accelerates campaign development, from ideation to execution, without sacrificing innovation or strategic alignment.

The Challenges of Traditional Campaign Development

The traditional approach to campaign development is rife with inefficiencies. Some common challenges include:

1. **Lengthy Brainstorming Processes**: Generating ideas through group discussions often takes time, with creative breakthroughs emerging only after multiple sessions.

2. **Resource Bottlenecks**: Creative teams, copywriters, and designers often face backlogs, delaying the production of campaign assets.

3. **Fragmented Workflows**: Coordinating between strategy, creative, and production teams can result in miscommunication and missed deadlines.

4. **Testing and Iteration**: Traditional A/B testing cycles can be time-consuming, delaying decisions about which messaging resonates best with audiences.

5. **Lack of Agility**: Campaigns designed months in advance may feel outdated by the time they launch, especially in industries driven by fast-moving trends.

These hurdles often lead to rushed campaigns, missed opportunities, and subpar results, underscoring the need for a more efficient approach.

How AI Accelerates Campaign Development

AI addresses these challenges by automating processes, enhancing collaboration, and providing real-time insights. Let's break down the key ways AI speeds up campaign development:

1. **Rapid Ideation**: AI tools like ChatGPT can generate creative ideas, slogans, and concepts within seconds based on detailed prompts. Marketers can input parameters such as target audience, tone, and campaign goals to receive tailored suggestions.

2. **Content Creation**: AI-driven tools can produce high-quality copy, visuals, and videos, reducing the time required to develop assets. For instance, AI can draft multiple versions of ad copy for A/B testing or generate templates for social media posts.

3. **Data-Driven Decision-Making**: AI analyzes historical data, audience behavior, and market trends to identify what works and what doesn't. This eliminates guesswork and ensures campaigns are built on a solid foundation of insights.

4. **Real-Time Testing and Optimization**: AI-powered platforms can run simultaneous tests across channels, analyzing performance in real time and recommending adjustments to improve engagement and conversion rates.

5. **Automated Workflows**: From scheduling social media posts to managing ad placements, AI streamlines operational tasks, allowing teams to focus on strategy and creativity.

AI-Powered Campaign Development Workflow

A typical AI-enabled campaign development process might look like this:

1. **Input and Ideation**:

o Teams define the campaign's objectives, target audience, and key messaging.

o Using AI, they generate multiple creative concepts, slogans, and content themes based on these inputs.

2. **Content Creation**:

o AI tools produce draft versions of ad copy, email templates, and social media posts.

o Visual AI platforms generate graphic designs, video templates, and animations aligned with the campaign's tone and branding.

3. **Testing and Feedback**:

o AI runs A/B tests on different content variations to identify what resonates most with the target audience.

o Real-time analytics provide insights into engagement metrics, click-through rates, and conversion rates.

4. **Refinement and Deployment**:

o Based on feedback, teams refine the campaign assets.

o AI automates the scheduling and distribution of content across channels, ensuring optimal timing and reach.

5. **Post-Campaign Analysis**:

o AI evaluates the campaign's performance, identifying areas of success and opportunities for improvement.

o Insights are stored for future campaigns, creating a feedback loop that enhances efficiency and effectiveness.

Case Study: AI Accelerating a Holiday Campaign

Imagine a retail brand preparing for a holiday campaign. Traditionally, this process might take weeks, involving brainstorming sessions, creative revisions, and manual scheduling. With AI, the timeline is dramatically compressed:

1. **Day 1: Ideation**

o The team uses AI to generate ideas for the campaign, focusing on themes like gifting, nostalgia, and family.

o AI proposes slogans such as "The Gift of Memories" and "Unwrap Joy This Season."

2. **Day 2: Content Creation**

o AI creates a library of social media posts, email copy, and ad variations.

o   Visual AI tools generate festive graphics and short video ads featuring product showcases.

3. **Day 3: Testing and Refinement**

o   AI runs A/B tests on email subject lines and social media captions, identifying the most engaging options.

o   Based on analytics, the team refines the messaging for maximum impact.

4. **Day 4: Launch and Optimization**

o   AI automates the scheduling of posts and ad placements across platforms.

o   Real-time monitoring allows the team to tweak the campaign mid-flight, reallocating budget to the best-performing channels.

5. **Post-Campaign**

o   AI analyzes the campaign's overall performance, providing insights into audience preferences and ROI.

By leveraging AI, the brand delivers a high-quality campaign in less than a week, maximizing its reach and relevance.

The Role of Prompt Engineering in Campaign Development

Prompt engineering is crucial for guiding AI in campaign development. Effective prompts enable marketers to extract creative and relevant outputs aligned with campaign goals.

- **Example 1: Ad Copy Creation**
  Prompt: "Generate three versions of ad copy for a skincare brand's summer campaign. The tone should be youthful and fun, emphasizing hydration and sun protection."

- **Example 2: Visual Concept Ideation**

  Prompt: "Suggest visual themes for a back-to-school campaign targeting parents of young children. Focus on warmth, family moments, and educational imagery."

- **Example 3: Real-Time Optimization**

  Prompt: "Analyze the performance of these two ad variations targeting eco-conscious consumers. Recommend which to scale and suggest improvements for the underperforming version."

Conclusion: The Future of Campaign Development with AI

AI has revolutionized campaign development, enabling marketers to move from concept to execution at unprecedented speed. By automating tedious tasks, generating creative ideas, and providing actionable insights, AI empowers teams to focus on strategy and storytelling.

As AI continues to evolve, its role in campaign development will only grow, enabling brands to adapt to market changes, connect with audiences more effectively, and deliver campaigns that are as timely as they are impactful. The future of marketing belongs to those who embrace AI as a creative and strategic partner.

The Double-Edged Sword of AI in Marketing

AI has undoubtedly transformed marketing ideation by offering unparalleled efficiency, creativity, and data-driven insights. However, like any tool, it comes with its challenges and limitations. These barriers can hinder its effectiveness and even lead to unintended consequences if not addressed properly.

While AI excels at generating ideas, producing content, and personalizing campaigns, it is not without its flaws. Issues such as lack of human intuition, ethical dilemmas, over-reliance on algorithms, and technological biases can pose significant challenges. Understanding these limitations is crucial for marketers to use AI effectively while recognizing where human expertise remains indispensable.

1. Lack of Human Creativity and Intuition

AI is a powerful tool for generating ideas based on patterns, trends, and prompts. However, it cannot replicate the uniquely human ability to think outside the box or understand abstract concepts.

- **Problem of Predictability**: AI-generated ideas often rely on existing data and past trends, which can result in ideas that feel formulaic or unoriginal.

- **Limited Context Awareness**: AI lacks deep cultural, emotional, and situational understanding, which can make it difficult to create campaigns that are nuanced or resonate deeply with specific audiences.

- **Missed "Eureka" Moments**: Human creativity often thrives on serendipity and unexpected connections, which AI cannot replicate.

For example, AI might suggest practical and data-supported ideas for a holiday campaign, but it might struggle to come up with a whimsical, culturally rich concept that surprises and delights audiences.

2. Dependence on Data Quality and Quantity

AI's performance depends entirely on the quality and quantity of the data it is trained on. If the data is incomplete, biased, or outdated, the outputs will reflect these flaws.

- **Bias in Training Data**: AI systems trained on biased datasets may perpetuate stereotypes or fail to understand diverse audiences. For example, an AI tool trained predominantly on Western consumer behavior may struggle to create campaigns for non-Western markets.

- **Data Gaps**: In niche industries or new markets where historical data is scarce, AI might generate irrelevant or uninformed ideas.

- **Over-Reliance on Historical Trends**: AI relies heavily on past data, which can limit its ability to predict or align with emerging trends that lack historical precedent.

To mitigate these issues, marketers must ensure data diversity, continuously update datasets, and supplement AI outputs with human oversight.

3. Ethical and Legal Challenges

As AI becomes more central to marketing, ethical and legal concerns arise, especially when it comes to privacy, intellectual property, and fairness.

- **Privacy Concerns**: AI often analyzes consumer behavior and personal data to generate insights. Mismanagement of this data can lead to privacy violations, eroding consumer trust.

- **Plagiarism Risks**: AI-generated content might unintentionally replicate existing ideas or phrases, raising questions of originality and intellectual property infringement.

- **Exploitation of Psychological Vulnerabilities**: AI's ability to target individuals based on behavioral data can lead to manipulative practices, such as exploiting consumer fears or insecurities.

Marketers must establish clear ethical guidelines, ensure compliance with data protection laws (e.g., GDPR, CCPA), and adopt a transparent approach to AI-driven campaigns.

4. Over-Reliance on Automation

While AI streamlines processes, over-reliance on it can stifle creativity, reduce adaptability, and introduce risks if the technology fails or produces flawed outputs.

- **Loss of Human Touch**: Automated campaigns may feel impersonal, lacking the emotional resonance of human-crafted messaging.

- **Blind Spots in Decision-Making**: AI tools may overlook critical contextual factors or outlier scenarios that humans would catch.

- **Reduced Critical Thinking**: Dependence on AI for ideation can discourage marketers from questioning assumptions or thinking critically about strategy and execution.

For example, an AI-driven campaign that works well for a majority audience may inadvertently alienate minority groups due to a lack of nuanced understanding.

5. Inability to Adapt to Rapid Cultural Shifts

AI struggles to keep pace with cultural shifts, social movements, and emerging societal values, particularly in real-time.

- **Static Knowledge Base**: Unless continuously updated, AI systems rely on outdated information that may not align with current trends or attitudes.

- **Difficulty with Context-Specific Sensitivity**: AI may fail to recognize sensitive or controversial topics, leading to tone-deaf or offensive campaign ideas.

- **Lagging Behind Viral Trends**: Rapidly evolving internet culture and social media trends often require the kind of quick, creative thinking that only humans can provide.

For example, during a social movement or global event, AI might not grasp the nuances needed to align messaging appropriately, potentially leading to public backlash.

6. High Implementation Costs and Learning Curves

Despite its long-term benefits, integrating AI into marketing ideation requires significant investment in tools, training, and infrastructure.

- **Cost Barriers**: Advanced AI platforms and the expertise to use them effectively can be prohibitively expensive for smaller organizations.

- **Training and Skill Development**: Teams must learn how to craft effective prompts, interpret AI-generated outputs, and integrate these insights into broader strategies.

- **Integration Challenges**: Aligning AI tools with existing workflows and systems can be time-consuming and disruptive.

Marketers must weigh the costs and benefits carefully, adopting AI incrementally while ensuring it complements, rather than replaces, human expertise.

7. Risk of Homogenization

As AI becomes more widely adopted, there is a risk that marketing campaigns will become homogenized, with many brands producing similar content based on similar datasets and algorithms.

- **Loss of Differentiation**: Overuse of AI-generated ideas may lead to a lack of originality, making it harder for brands to stand out in crowded markets.

- **Algorithmic Convergence**: AI tools trained on similar data often produce similar outputs, resulting in a "sameness" across campaigns.

For example, if multiple brands in the same industry use AI to generate social media posts, the resulting content might feel repetitive and uninspired to consumers.

The Need for Balance

While AI offers transformative potential for marketing ideation, its challenges and limitations must not be overlooked. By understanding these pitfalls, marketers can take proactive steps to address them, ensuring that AI enhances, rather than hinders, the creative process.

The key lies in balancing the efficiency and scalability of AI with the intuition, creativity, and cultural awareness that only humans can provide. By combining the strengths of both, brands can navigate the complexities of modern marketing while maintaining authenticity, innovation, and ethical integrity.

A New Era for Marketing

The future of marketing is inextricably linked to the evolution of artificial intelligence (AI). As AI technologies continue to mature, they promise to redefine how brands connect with their audiences, shape consumer experiences, and drive business growth. From predictive analytics and hyper-personalized content to voice-activated commerce and immersive virtual experiences, AI is poised to create unprecedented opportunities for innovation.

However, with these advancements come critical questions: How will marketers maintain authenticity in an increasingly automated world? What ethical challenges will arise, and how can they be addressed? This chapter explores the transformative potential of AI in marketing, the emerging trends shaping the industry, and the strategies brands can adopt to thrive in an AI-driven future.

1. Hyper-Personalization at Scale

The ability to deliver personalized experiences has been a cornerstone of effective marketing, and AI is set to take this to an entirely new level.

- **Dynamic Content Customization**: AI can analyze individual consumer preferences, behavior, and demographics in real time to create highly tailored messages. For instance, streaming platforms like Netflix already use AI to recommend content based on viewing history, a trend that will expand to other industries.

- **Predictive Consumer Insights**: Advanced algorithms can anticipate consumer needs before they are even expressed, enabling brands to proactively offer solutions.

- **One-to-One Marketing**: AI will make it feasible to create unique experiences for each customer at scale, such as personalized product recommendations, custom email campaigns, and targeted ads.

Brands that embrace hyper-personalization will build deeper connections with their audiences, leading to increased loyalty and higher conversion rates.

2. AI-Powered Creativity and Campaign Development

The integration of AI into creative processes will redefine how campaigns are conceptualized, designed, and executed.

- **AI-Generated Visuals and Copy**: Tools like generative AI are already capable of creating visually stunning graphics, videos, and written content. In the future, these capabilities will become even more refined, producing content that is indistinguishable from human-created materials.

- **Collaborative Creativity**: AI will act as a creative collaborator, providing suggestions, generating concepts, and optimizing content based on performance data.

- **Real-Time Campaign Adjustments**: AI will enable marketers to adjust live campaigns on the fly, using data-driven insights to optimize performance in real time.

This shift will not only accelerate the creative process but also ensure that campaigns are more targeted, relevant, and impactful.

3. Voice and Conversational AI

As voice-activated technologies like smart speakers and virtual assistants become ubiquitous, they will play a pivotal role in the future of marketing.

- **Voice Search Optimization**: Brands will need to adapt their content for voice search, focusing on conversational queries and natural language processing (NLP).

- **Voice Commerce**: Consumers are increasingly using voice commands to shop, making it essential for brands to integrate with platforms like Alexa, Google Assistant, and Siri.

- **Conversational Engagement**: AI-powered chatbots and virtual assistants will enable brands to interact with customers in a conversational, human-like manner, providing instant support and recommendations.

The rise of voice and conversational AI will create new opportunities for engagement while challenging marketers to rethink how they design and deliver messages.

4. Immersive Experiences with AI and AR/VR

The convergence of AI with augmented reality (AR) and virtual reality (VR) will redefine experiential marketing, creating immersive, interactive campaigns that captivate audiences.

- **Virtual Try-Ons**: AI-powered AR applications will allow consumers to visualize products in their own environments, from trying on clothing to previewing furniture in their homes.

- **Immersive Brand Storytelling**: VR experiences will enable brands to transport consumers into virtual worlds, creating unforgettable stories and emotional connections.

- **AI-Powered Personalization in AR/VR**: By analyzing user preferences, AI will tailor immersive experiences to individual tastes, enhancing engagement and satisfaction.

These technologies will blur the line between digital and physical marketing, offering brands new ways to inspire and delight consumers.

5. Ethical and Responsible AI in Marketing

As AI becomes more embedded in marketing, ethical considerations will take center stage.

- **Data Privacy and Security**: With AI relying heavily on consumer data, brands must prioritize transparency and compliance with regulations like GDPR and CCPA.

- **Bias and Fairness**: Marketers must address biases in AI algorithms to ensure that campaigns are inclusive and equitable.

- **Consumer Trust**: Over-reliance on AI or intrusive personalization could lead to consumer pushback. Maintaining authenticity and respecting boundaries will be critical.

- **Sustainability**: AI-driven marketing must align with broader corporate social responsibility (CSR) initiatives, such as minimizing the environmental impact of digital campaigns.

The future of AI-driven marketing will hinge on finding a balance between innovation and ethical responsibility.

6. The Evolving Role of Marketers in an AI-Driven World

As AI takes over routine tasks and analytics, the role of marketers will shift from execution to strategy, creativity, and relationship-building.

- **Strategic Oversight**: Marketers will focus on guiding AI systems, setting objectives, and ensuring alignment with brand values.

- **Human-AI Collaboration**: The most successful marketers will be those who can effectively collaborate with AI, leveraging its capabilities while infusing campaigns with human insight and emotion.

- **Continuous Learning**: As AI technologies evolve, marketers will need to stay ahead by developing new skills, such as prompt engineering, data interpretation, and ethical decision-making.

The future marketer will be a hybrid professional, blending technical expertise with creativity, empathy, and strategic vision.

7. Preparing for the Future

To thrive in an AI-driven marketing landscape, brands must take proactive steps today:

- **Invest in AI Tools**: Adopt cutting-edge AI platforms that align with your business goals and scale with your needs.

- **Build AI Expertise**: Train teams to use AI effectively, from crafting prompts to interpreting analytics.

- **Prioritize Ethical AI**: Develop clear guidelines for ethical AI use, focusing on transparency, inclusivity, and consumer trust.

- **Foster Innovation**: Encourage a culture of experimentation, where teams can explore new ways to integrate AI into marketing strategies.

By taking these steps, brands can position themselves as leaders in the next wave of marketing innovation.

Embracing the AI Revolution

The future of AI-driven marketing is both exciting and transformative. With the potential to deliver hyper-personalized experiences, revolutionize creative processes, and enhance consumer engagement, AI will become an indispensable tool for brands.

However, success will depend on how well marketers navigate its challenges, balance innovation with ethics, and embrace their evolving roles in a technology-driven world. By harnessing the power of AI while maintaining a human touch, brands can not only survive but thrive in the dynamic landscape of future marketing.

Part 3: Advanced AI Brainstorming Techniques

Using AI for Collaborative Creativity

The process of brainstorming has long been a cornerstone of innovation, yet traditional methods often fall short in today's fast-paced, complex work environments. Dominant voices can overshadow quieter participants, groupthink may stifle originality, and the sheer volume of ideas can overwhelm rather than inspire. In this context, integrating AI into team brainstorming offers a transformative opportunity to overcome these challenges and unlock the collective creativity of diverse groups.

AI serves as a neutral, tireless, and efficient facilitator, capable of generating, organizing, and refining ideas at a scale unimaginable with conventional approaches. By leveraging AI, teams can democratize the brainstorming process, ensuring that every perspective is heard and every contribution valued. This introduction explores how AI redefines team brainstorming and sets the stage for the actionable strategies outlined in this chapter.

The Pitfalls of Traditional Brainstorming

Traditional brainstorming methods often struggle to deliver optimal results, particularly in group settings where dynamics can hinder creativity:

1. **Dominant Participants:** Strong personalities or authority figures can unintentionally monopolize discussions, limiting input from others.

2. **Idea Fatigue:** Teams often experience diminishing returns after initial bursts of creativity, leading to repetitive or shallow suggestions.

3. **Groupthink:** The desire for consensus can suppress unconventional or dissenting ideas.

4. **Time Constraints:** In live sessions, teams may struggle to explore ideas deeply due to limited time.

These issues underscore the need for tools and methods that enhance inclusivity, structure, and productivity in brainstorming sessions.

AI as a Neutral Facilitator

AI addresses many of the limitations inherent in traditional brainstorming by acting as a neutral, unbiased participant in the creative process. Its unique strengths include:

- **Generating Diverse Ideas:** AI can produce a wide range of suggestions based on prompts, ensuring that teams start with a rich pool of possibilities.

- **Amplifying Inclusivity:** By processing contributions anonymously, AI helps level the playing field, allowing all voices to be heard equally.

- **Streamlining Organization:** AI tools can cluster related ideas, highlight trends, and categorize inputs, making it easier to identify actionable insights.

- **Encouraging Iteration:** Unlike human participants who may tire or lose focus, AI can continuously refine and expand ideas without fatigue.

The Benefits of AI-Driven Team Brainstorming

By incorporating AI, teams can achieve a higher level of efficiency, creativity, and alignment:

- **Efficiency:** AI accelerates the brainstorming process by quickly generating ideas, organizing them, and identifying patterns.

- **Creativity:** AI introduces unexpected perspectives and novel combinations, pushing teams to think beyond conventional boundaries.

- **Alignment:** Through structured prompts and categorization, AI helps teams focus on shared goals and integrate diverse inputs into cohesive strategies.

Overview of This Chapter

This chapter provides a comprehensive guide to leveraging AI in team brainstorming sessions. It explores:

1. The foundational role of AI in enhancing collaborative creativity.

2. Practical steps for preparing and executing AI-facilitated brainstorming sessions.

3. Techniques for crafting effective prompts that align team contributions with project objectives.

4. Strategies for synthesizing diverse ideas into unified plans.

5. Real-world examples and an interactive exercise to help readers apply these concepts in their own teams.

AI doesn't replace human ingenuity; rather, it amplifies and enhances it. As we delve deeper into this chapter, you'll discover how to seamlessly integrate AI into your team's creative processes, transforming brainstorming sessions into powerful engines of innovation. Let's begin by understanding the foundational role of AI in collaborative creativity.

The Role of AI in Collaborative Creativity

Collaboration thrives on diversity—of perspectives, ideas, and problem-solving approaches. However, managing and harnessing this diversity in a structured way can be challenging in team brainstorming sessions. AI, as a collaborative partner, provides a unique opportunity to act as a facilitator, idea generator, and organizer, empowering teams to navigate the complexities of group dynamics while fostering creativity.

This section explores how AI can enhance collaborative creativity, focusing on its ability to democratize contributions, stimulate innovative thinking, and bridge gaps in understanding among team members.

AI as a Creative Equalizer

One of AI's most valuable roles in collaboration is its capacity to level the playing field. Traditional brainstorming sessions often struggle with issues such as:

- **Uneven Participation:** Introverted or less confident team members may hesitate to share ideas.

- **Bias and Judgment:** Fear of criticism can stifle innovative or unconventional suggestions.

AI mitigates these issues by serving as an unbiased intermediary, enabling anonymous contributions and ensuring that all ideas are considered based on merit rather than their source. This creates an inclusive environment where every team member feels empowered to participate.

AI as an Infinite Idea Generator

The creative potential of AI lies in its ability to analyze vast datasets and generate ideas that might not occur naturally to human teams. It can:

- **Introduce Novel Perspectives:** AI can suggest unconventional approaches or draw from unrelated fields to inspire innovative thinking.

- **Avoid Repetition:** By analyzing previous discussions or data, AI helps avoid redundant suggestions, keeping the brainstorming session dynamic and productive.

- **Support Iterative Creativity:** Teams can refine ideas by repeatedly prompting the AI, exploring variations and alternatives until the best solutions emerge.

AI as a Knowledge Bridge

Teams often consist of individuals with varying expertise and viewpoints. While diversity enhances creativity, it can also lead to misunderstandings or misalignment. AI helps bridge these gaps by:

- **Synthesizing Complex Information:** AI can distill large amounts of input into clear, concise summaries, ensuring that all team members are on the same page.

- **Facilitating Communication:** By acting as a translator between technical and non-technical stakeholders, AI ensures that ideas are accessible to everyone involved.

- **Highlighting Patterns and Trends:** AI tools can identify common themes in team input, making it easier to align contributions with project goals.

AI as a Catalyst for Divergent and Convergent Thinking

Creative collaboration involves both divergent thinking (generating a wide range of ideas) and convergent thinking (narrowing them down to actionable solutions). AI excels in supporting both processes:

1. **Divergent Thinking:** AI can generate a high volume of diverse ideas quickly, sparking inspiration and expanding the creative landscape.

2. **Convergent Thinking:** AI can help teams evaluate, categorize, and prioritize ideas, streamlining the decision-making process.

For example, an AI tool might generate 50 potential product features based on a prompt and then categorize them into themes like usability, cost-effectiveness, and innovation. The team can then focus on the most promising categories, ensuring alignment with strategic objectives.

AI and Human Synergy

While AI is a powerful tool for enhancing creativity, its true value lies in its partnership with human ingenuity. AI brings speed, scale, and objectivity, but it is the human team that provides emotional intelligence, intuition, and contextual understanding. Together, they form a synergistic relationship that drives collaborative creativity to new heights.

Key aspects of this synergy include:

- **Iterative Refinement:** Humans and AI collaborate to refine and improve ideas, leveraging the strengths of both.

- **Emotional Resonance:** Humans bring empathy and cultural awareness to ensure ideas resonate with the target audience.

- **Judgment and Ethics:** Human oversight ensures that AI-generated ideas align with ethical and organizational values.

AI transforms team brainstorming by enhancing inclusivity, stimulating creativity, and fostering alignment. Its ability to generate diverse ideas, bridge knowledge gaps, and balance divergent and convergent thinking makes it an invaluable partner in collaborative creativity. However, the magic happens when AI and humans work together, each amplifying the other's strengths.

Setting the Stage for AI-Enhanced Team Sessions

Integrating AI into team brainstorming requires preparation, structure, and a clear vision to maximize its potential. A successful AI-enhanced session depends on how well the environment is tailored for collaboration and how effectively the team engages with the AI tools. This section outlines actionable steps to prepare for and execute productive, AI-driven team brainstorming sessions.

1. Define the Purpose and Goals

Every brainstorming session should begin with clarity of purpose. Teams must agree on what they aim to achieve and how AI will support those goals. Clear objectives ensure focused discussion and help the AI generate relevant and actionable ideas.

Key Actions:

- Identify the **primary goal**: Are you solving a problem, innovating a product, or exploring new opportunities?

- Break goals into **specific questions** or prompts for the AI to address.

- Set **metrics for success**, such as the number of actionable ideas generated or a clearer understanding of a challenge.

  Example Goal: Develop three innovative product features to enhance user experience.

2. Choose the Right Tools and Platforms

Selecting the appropriate AI tools tailored to the session's goals is critical. Different tools excel in various areas, from generating creative ideas to synthesizing input from large teams.

Considerations for Tool Selection:

- **Ease of Use:** Ensure the tool is intuitive and accessible to all team members.

- **Capabilities:** Match the tool's features with the session's needs (e.g., text generation, data analysis, or visual brainstorming).

- **Integration:** Use tools that seamlessly integrate with collaboration platforms like Slack, Microsoft Teams, or Miro.

Examples of Tools:

- **ChatGPT or Bard:** Idea generation and iteration.

- **Miro:** Visual collaboration and mapping AI-generated ideas.

- **Notion AI:** Organizing and summarizing team input.

3. Prepare the Team

Before diving into the session, it's crucial to align team members on the role of AI and how to interact with it effectively. This helps manage expectations and ensures productive engagement.

Key Actions:

- **Educate the Team:** Provide a brief overview of how the AI will be used and its capabilities.

- **Set Collaboration Norms:** Establish guidelines for engaging with the AI and one another (e.g., active participation, respect for all ideas).

- **Address Concerns:** Reassure the team that AI complements, not replaces, human creativity.

Example Introduction:

"AI will serve as a facilitator in our brainstorming session. It's here to generate ideas, identify patterns, and help us explore new perspectives. Our role is to guide it, refine its outputs, and bring our expertise to the table."

4. Craft a Structured Agenda

A well-structured agenda ensures the session remains focused and productive. Incorporate AI-driven activities at key points while leaving room for human interaction and discussion.

Sample Agenda:

1. **Introduction (10 mins):** Outline goals, introduce the AI tool, and explain the session flow.

2. **Divergent Thinking Phase (20 mins):** Use AI to generate a broad range of ideas based on prompts.

3. **Discussion and Refinement (20 mins):** Review AI outputs and refine ideas collaboratively.

4. **Convergent Thinking Phase (20 mins):** Use AI to categorize and prioritize ideas based on team input.

5. **Wrap-Up (10 mins):** Summarize key takeaways and agree on next steps.

5. Create Engaging Prompts

The quality of AI outputs depends on the quality of prompts. Craft prompts that are specific, contextual, and aligned with the session's goals.

Tips for Effective Prompts:

- Start with **open-ended questions**: "What are some innovative features for a digital fitness app?"

- Provide **context**: "Considering trends in gamification, what features could improve engagement for users aged 20-35?"

- Use iterative prompts: "Can you build on the following idea by adding more detail or alternatives?"

Example:

Prompt: "Generate three customer-centric features for a fitness app aimed at Gen Z, focusing on personalization and community engagement."

6. Set the Right Environment

A conducive environment encourages creativity and focus. For AI-enhanced sessions, ensure that both the physical and digital spaces support seamless collaboration.

Key Considerations:

- **Physical Space:** Provide a comfortable setting with minimal distractions, equipped with necessary technology.

- **Digital Tools:** Ensure all participants have access to the AI tool and any collaborative platforms.

- **Facilitator Role:** Assign a facilitator to guide the session, manage time, and keep discussions aligned with goals.

7. Foster Iterative Feedback Loops

AI-driven sessions thrive on iteration. Encourage the team to continuously refine AI-generated ideas and provide feedback to improve outputs.

Steps for Iteration:

1. Review initial outputs together.

2. Identify strengths and weaknesses in the AI's suggestions.

3. Re-prompt the AI with more specific guidance or additional context.

Example Iterative Process:

- **First Prompt:** "Suggest strategies for increasing customer retention in e-commerce."

- **Follow-Up Prompt:** "Focus on subscription models and loyalty programs, considering small-to-medium businesses."

Preparing for AI-enhanced team brainstorming requires careful planning and thoughtful execution. By defining clear goals, selecting the right tools, and crafting engaging prompts, teams can create an environment where AI acts as a powerful catalyst for collaboration. Combined with structured agendas and iterative feedback, these strategies set the stage for creativity to flourish in new and transformative ways.

Designing Effective Prompts for Team Brainstorming

Prompts are the bridge between human creativity and AI's potential to amplify it. A well-designed prompt ensures that the AI provides outputs that are relevant, diverse, and actionable. Crafting prompts for team brainstorming requires precision, clarity, and an understanding of the session's goals. This section provides a guide for creating prompts that foster collaboration, generate innovative ideas, and align diverse perspectives into cohesive plans.

1. The Anatomy of an Effective Prompt

An effective prompt is clear, goal-oriented, and contextually rich. It provides AI with enough direction to generate useful outputs while leaving room for creativity.

Key Elements of a Prompt:

- **Objective:** Clearly state the purpose of the prompt.
- Example: "Generate ideas for improving employee engagement in remote teams."

- **Context:** Provide background or relevant details to guide the AI.

o   Example: "Considering trends in flexible work policies, suggest initiatives that cater to diverse employee needs."

- **Constraints:** Define parameters or limits for the AI's response.

o   Example: "Focus on cost-effective strategies suitable for small businesses."

- **Tone and Style:** Specify the desired tone or approach for the output.

o   Example: "Generate ideas in a conversational tone suitable for a brainstorming session."

2. Types of Prompts for Team Brainstorming

Different phases of brainstorming call for varied types of prompts. Tailor prompts to the team's needs at each stage.

a. Divergent Thinking Prompts
Encourage the generation of a wide range of ideas without judgment or prioritization.

- Example: "List five unconventional solutions for reducing carbon footprints in urban areas."

- Example: "Brainstorm ways to integrate AI into daily retail operations to enhance customer experience."

b. Convergent Thinking Prompts
Focus on narrowing down ideas, identifying patterns, or prioritizing options.

- Example: "Group these ideas into three categories based on feasibility and potential impact."

- Example: "From the following suggestions, identify the top two that align with our company's sustainability goals."

c. Refinement Prompts
Ask the AI to improve or elaborate on existing ideas.

- Example: "Expand on this idea by adding specific steps for implementation."

- Example: "Provide pros and cons for using gamification in this customer engagement strategy."

d. Integrative Prompts
Align diverse perspectives or unify multiple ideas into a cohesive plan.

- Example: "Combine the following ideas into a single comprehensive proposal."

- Example: "Suggest a framework for integrating these features into a user-friendly product."

3. Techniques for Prompt Optimization

Prompts often need to be refined to achieve the desired output. Use these techniques to craft better prompts:

a. Ask Specific Questions
Avoid vague prompts that lead to generic responses. Be as specific as possible to guide the AI effectively.

- **Weak Prompt:** "Suggest ways to improve team productivity."

- **Improved Prompt:** "Suggest three productivity tools for remote teams to enhance collaboration and reduce meeting fatigue."

b. Add Constraints

Constraints focus the AI's responses and make them more actionable.

- Example: "Generate five low-cost marketing ideas for a startup targeting Gen Z customers."

c. Use Iterative Prompts

Start with a broad prompt and refine it based on the initial response.

- **Initial Prompt:** "Suggest ways to enhance customer loyalty for an e-commerce platform."

- **Follow-Up Prompt:** "Focus on subscription services and personalized recommendations for premium members."

d. Encourage Creative Thinking

Phrase prompts in a way that invites out-of-the-box ideas.

- Example: "Imagine you're designing a product for the year 2050. What features would it include?"

4. Engaging the Team with Prompts

AI prompts should not replace human input but rather serve as a springboard for discussion. Encourage the team to interact with AI-generated outputs to foster collaboration.

Collaborative Prompt Techniques:

- **Open Feedback:** Share AI outputs with the team and invite feedback.

- Example: "The AI suggested these five ideas. What resonates with you, and how can we improve them?"

- **Comparative Prompts:** Present multiple AI-generated options and ask the team to compare or prioritize.

- Example: "Which of these two strategies do you think aligns better with our brand identity?"

- **Challenge Prompts:** Use the AI to play devil's advocate by critiquing ideas.

- Example: "List potential risks or drawbacks for implementing this strategy."

5. Examples of Effective Prompts

Below are sample prompts tailored to common brainstorming scenarios:

Scenario 1: Product Innovation

- "Generate three innovative features for a fitness app targeting busy professionals."

- "Suggest ways to integrate augmented reality into an online learning platform for children."

Scenario 2: Process Improvement

- "Identify three strategies for streamlining the onboarding process for new employees."

- "Suggest cost-saving measures for a supply chain in the manufacturing sector."

Scenario 3: Marketing Strategy

- "Propose a social media campaign to promote a sustainable fashion brand."

- "Develop an email marketing strategy to re-engage inactive customers."

6. Tools and Techniques for Real-Time Prompt Refinement

During live brainstorming sessions, teams may need to refine prompts in real-time based on AI outputs.

Strategies for Real-Time Refinement:

- **Collaborative Iteration:** Involve the team in rephrasing prompts to achieve better results.

o Example: "How can we adjust this prompt to focus more on customer retention?"

- **AI Feedback:** Use the AI to critique its own output.

o Example: "Identify any gaps or areas for improvement in the following ideas."

- **Rapid Prototyping:** Combine quick AI iterations with immediate team input to build on ideas dynamically.

Best Practices for Integrating AI into Sessions

Integrating AI into brainstorming and collaborative creativity sessions can elevate team productivity, foster innovation, and streamline the ideation process. However, successful integration requires intentional design, effective facilitation, and a clear understanding of AI's role as an enabler rather than a replacement for human creativity. This section outlines best practices to ensure AI contributes meaningfully to your sessions.

1. Define the Goals of the Session

Clearly articulate the purpose of the brainstorming session before integrating AI. This helps set expectations and ensures that AI outputs align with the session's objectives.

Key Questions to Address:

- What specific outcomes do we want from this session?

o Example: Generate a list of new product ideas, refine an existing strategy, or address a specific challenge.

- How will AI support the team?

o Example: As a creativity booster, pattern recognizer, or summarizer of ideas.

2. Select the Right AI Tools

Not all AI tools are suited for every type of brainstorming. Choose tools that align with your goals and integrate seamlessly with your team's workflow.

Considerations When Choosing AI Tools:

- **Capabilities:** Ensure the AI tool supports ideation, analysis, or organization based on your needs.

- **User-Friendliness:** Select tools that are intuitive and require minimal training.

- **Customization:** Opt for tools that allow customization of prompts and outputs.

- **Integration:** Prefer tools that integrate with your existing collaboration platforms (e.g., Slack, Microsoft Teams).

3. Establish Roles for AI and Humans

Define the role of AI in the session to avoid confusion or over-reliance. AI should complement human creativity, not overshadow it.

Possible AI Roles:

- Idea Generator: Provide raw ideas for the team to refine.

- Pattern Recognizer: Identify trends or recurring themes in team discussions.

- Gap Finder: Highlight areas that need further exploration.

- Summarizer: Condense discussions into actionable points.

Human Roles:

- Facilitator: Guides the session and integrates AI outputs into discussions.

- Analyst: Evaluates the relevance and feasibility of AI suggestions.

- Refiner: Enhances AI-generated ideas with team insights.

4. Prepare the Team for AI Collaboration

Educate the team about the role of AI and set expectations for its contributions. Encourage an open mindset to foster collaboration between humans and AI.

Best Practices for Team Preparation:

- **Introduce the Tool:** Briefly explain how the AI works and its capabilities.

- **Set Expectations:** Clarify that AI is an aid, not a decision-maker.

- **Address Concerns:** Discuss potential biases or limitations of the AI.

- **Encourage Engagement:** Promote active participation in refining AI outputs.

5. Facilitate an Inclusive Session

Ensure all participants, regardless of their comfort level with AI, feel valued and included in the session.

Tips for Inclusivity:

- Balance AI inputs with human contributions to avoid overshadowing individual creativity.

- Use AI outputs as starting points for discussions, not definitive answers.

- Encourage all team members to critique and build upon AI-generated ideas.

6. Use AI Strategically During the Session

Incorporate AI at the right moments to maximize its impact without disrupting the flow of the session.

When to Use AI:

- **Kickoff:** Generate initial ideas to spark creativity.

o Example: "AI, list five potential solutions to this challenge based on industry trends."

- **Mid-Session:** Identify patterns or gaps in ongoing discussions.

o Example: "Summarize the team's suggestions so far and highlight unexplored areas."

- **Wrap-Up:** Synthesize key takeaways and create actionable next steps.

o Example: "AI, consolidate our top ideas into a summary with pros and cons."

7. Iterate and Refine AI Outputs

AI-generated ideas are often a starting point, not the final product. Work collaboratively to refine these outputs into actionable plans.

Steps for Refining AI Outputs:

- **Evaluate:** Assess the relevance and feasibility of AI suggestions.

- **Build On:** Combine AI ideas with team insights to create comprehensive solutions.

- **Test:** Pilot AI-driven ideas in small-scale scenarios to validate their effectiveness.

8. Monitor and Address Bias

AI outputs can reflect biases present in its training data. Regularly monitor outputs to ensure they are inclusive, unbiased, and relevant.

Strategies to Mitigate Bias:

- Use diverse and inclusive datasets when training custom AI models.

- Encourage the team to critique AI suggestions critically.

- Provide feedback to the AI by refining prompts or flagging biased responses.

9. Foster a Feedback Loop

Establish a continuous improvement cycle by collecting feedback on AI's performance and the overall session.

Collecting Feedback:

- Ask participants about the effectiveness of AI in the session.

o Example: "Did AI outputs help generate better ideas or insights?"

- Identify areas where AI integration could be improved.

o Example: "What challenges did you face when working with the AI tool?"

- Update prompts and session designs based on feedback to enhance future sessions.

10. Encourage Post-Session Reflection

Leverage AI to summarize key takeaways and support team reflection after the session.

Post-Session Actions:

- Share AI-generated summaries or reports with participants.

- Use AI to identify recurring themes or long-term opportunities from multiple sessions.

- Encourage the team to provide feedback on AI's contribution to outcomes.

Aligning Diverse Ideas into Unified Plans

One of the greatest challenges in brainstorming sessions is synthesizing diverse, and sometimes conflicting, ideas into a coherent and actionable plan. AI can play a pivotal role in facilitating this process by analyzing input, identifying patterns, and offering summaries. However, the human touch remains crucial to ensure that the resulting plan reflects the team's goals, values, and creativity. This section outlines strategies and best practices for using AI to align diverse perspectives into a unified plan.

1. Recognizing the Value of Diversity

Diverse ideas arise from unique backgrounds, expertise, and perspectives, enriching the brainstorming process. However, aligning these inputs requires a balance between inclusivity and focus. AI tools can assist by organizing ideas into categories, spotlighting common themes, and surfacing connections that might not be immediately apparent.

Steps to Harness Diversity:

- **Encourage Open Contribution:** Use AI to anonymously collect ideas, fostering equitable participation.

- **Analyze for Overlaps:** Use clustering algorithms or AI tools to group similar ideas.

o   Example: "AI, categorize these suggestions based on their focus area (e.g., customer experience, cost efficiency)."

- **Celebrate Outliers:** Highlight unique ideas that may offer disruptive innovation.

2. Structuring the Alignment Process

To bring diverse ideas together, structure the session in phases that encourage exploration, refinement, and consensus-building. AI's ability to assist with sorting and prioritizing inputs enhances efficiency and focus.

Suggested Workflow:

1. **Ideation Phase:** Use AI to generate or collect a wide range of ideas.

2. **Categorization Phase:** Let AI cluster or tag ideas based on keywords or themes.

3. **Evaluation Phase:** Apply scoring mechanisms (e.g., feasibility, impact) to rank ideas with AI assistance.

4. **Synthesis Phase:** Collaborate with AI to merge complementary ideas into cohesive strategies.

5. **Validation Phase:** Use AI to simulate or predict outcomes of the proposed plan.

3. Designing Effective AI Prompts for Alignment

Crafting precise prompts for AI can streamline the process of merging diverse ideas. Well-designed prompts encourage the AI to focus on commonalities, while respecting the nuances of individual inputs.

Examples of Effective Prompts:

- "Identify common themes in these suggestions and group them into three categories."

- "Combine these ideas into a single strategy that emphasizes customer satisfaction and cost savings."

- "Highlight potential conflicts between these suggestions and propose ways to resolve them."

Tips for Prompt Optimization:

- Be specific: Clearly state the desired outcome (e.g., categories, summaries, or conflicts).

- Contextualize: Provide background information or constraints to guide the AI's response.

- Iterate: Refine prompts based on initial outputs to improve accuracy and relevance.

4. Bridging Contradictory Ideas

When team members' ideas conflict, AI can act as an impartial mediator by objectively analyzing the pros and cons of each perspective.

Strategies for Resolving Conflicts:

- **Propose Compromises:**

  o Example: "AI, find a middle ground between prioritizing innovation and minimizing costs in these ideas."

- **Highlight Mutual Benefits:**

o Example: "Identify shared goals or outcomes between these opposing strategies."

- **Simulate Scenarios:** Use AI to model potential outcomes for conflicting approaches, allowing the team to make data-informed decisions.

5. Creating a Unified Plan

With AI's assistance, transform categorized and refined ideas into a structured, actionable plan. The AI can draft outlines, prioritize steps, and suggest resource allocations, enabling the team to focus on decision-making and execution.

Steps to Craft the Plan:

1. **Prioritize Objectives:** Use AI to rank ideas based on alignment with goals, feasibility, and impact.

2. **Draft the Framework:**

o Example: "AI, create a high-level plan that incorporates these key ideas."

3. **Refine with Feedback:** Present the draft to the team for further input and adjustments.

4. **Finalize the Plan:** Use AI to consolidate feedback into the final document, ensuring clarity and coherence.

6. Leveraging Visualization Tools

AI-powered visualization tools can present complex information in a more digestible format, aiding the team in understanding and aligning diverse inputs.

Common Visualization Techniques:

- **Mind Maps:** Show the relationships between ideas.

- **Heat Maps:** Highlight high-priority or high-impact ideas.

- **Flowcharts:** Illustrate the sequence of steps in the unified plan.

Tool Recommendations:

- **Miro:** For interactive mind mapping and collaboration.

- **Lucidchart:** For creating detailed workflows and flowcharts.

- **AI-Enhanced Platforms:** Such as Notion AI for generating summaries with embedded visuals.

7. Balancing AI Suggestions with Human Insights

While AI excels in pattern recognition and efficiency, human intuition and creativity are critical for ensuring the unified plan resonates with the team's vision and organizational values.

Balancing Strategies:

- Use AI outputs as a starting point for discussions.

- Empower team members to critique and enhance AI-generated suggestions.

- Regularly revisit the plan to incorporate new ideas or address emerging challenges.

8. Refining Through Iteration

Iterative refinement ensures the unified plan remains robust and relevant. AI can assist by tracking progress, analyzing feedback, and suggesting adjustments.

Continuous Improvement Cycle:

1. Implement the plan in stages.

2. Collect data and feedback on outcomes.

3. Use AI to analyze results and propose optimizations.

4. Update the plan based on insights gained.

Real-World Examples of AI-Enhanced Collaborative Creativity

Exploring how organizations and teams leverage AI to align diverse ideas into unified strategies offers valuable insights into practical applications. The following real-world examples illustrate how businesses have successfully integrated AI into collaborative brainstorming and planning processes.

1. IBM: Watson as a Creative Partner

IBM has integrated its AI system, Watson, into collaborative innovation processes to assist teams in generating and refining ideas. For example:

- **Scenario:** A product development team at IBM used Watson to analyze customer feedback from multiple channels and generate ideas for new product features.

- **AI's Role:**

o Analyzed vast amounts of unstructured data (reviews, surveys, social media).

- Identified recurring themes and potential customer needs.

- Suggested innovative solutions based on predictive models and market trends.

- **Outcome:** Watson enabled the team to prioritize features that resonated most with customers, ensuring alignment across marketing, design, and development departments.

2. Procter & Gamble: Virtual Collaboration with AI

Procter & Gamble (P&G), a global leader in consumer goods, has adopted AI tools to enhance virtual brainstorming and streamline decision-making across geographically dispersed teams.

- **Scenario:** Teams working on a new skincare line used AI to:

- Combine diverse perspectives from R&D, marketing, and consumer insights.

- Cluster ideas into themes such as sustainability, effectiveness, and affordability.

- Simulate customer reactions using AI-driven predictive analytics.

- **AI's Role:**

- Aggregated and categorized input from participants in real-time.

- Provided instant feedback on market feasibility and competitive positioning.

- **Outcome:** The resulting plan aligned innovative formulations with customer preferences, reducing development time and increasing market readiness.

3. Google: AI in Cross-Functional Collaboration

Google has pioneered AI-powered collaboration tools such as **Google Workspace AI** to enhance creative processes within teams.

- **Scenario:** The Google Ads team used AI tools to align ideas across diverse functional areas, including engineering, sales, and customer support.

- **AI's Role:**

    o Summarized brainstorming sessions and highlighted recurring ideas.

    o Suggested potential product features based on market analytics and past user behavior.

    o Provided real-time translations to ensure inclusivity in multinational teams.

- **Outcome:** AI facilitated a cohesive vision for the product roadmap, reducing iteration cycles and fostering team alignment.

4. Nike: Creating Personalized Consumer Experiences

Nike has used AI-driven collaboration tools to generate innovative marketing strategies for personalized consumer experiences.

- **Scenario:** The marketing and tech teams brainstormed ways to enhance the Nike app's personalization features.

- **AI's Role:**

  o Mapped diverse inputs from team members into clear consumer personas.

  o Identified gaps in the existing customer journey.

  o Proposed actionable steps to incorporate AR technology and gamification into the app.

- **Outcome:** The resulting unified plan increased app engagement and improved customer retention rates.

5. Lego: Crowdsourcing and AI for Product Development

Lego has integrated AI with its crowdsourcing platform, **Lego Ideas**, to facilitate collaborative creativity between its community and internal teams.

- **Scenario:** Lego collected thousands of product suggestions from fans and used AI to process the submissions.

- **AI's Role:**

  o Analyzed fan submissions for originality, feasibility, and alignment with Lego's brand.

  o Highlighted ideas with strong potential for market success.

  o Assisted in merging similar ideas into unified concepts.

- **Outcome:** AI-enabled collaboration resulted in innovative product lines, such as the **Lego Women of NASA** set, which became a bestseller and strengthened the brand's market position.

6. Spotify: AI-Driven Team Ideation for Playlists

Spotify's teams use AI to brainstorm new features for playlist personalization and curation.

- **Scenario:** A cross-functional team worked on a feature to improve user-generated playlists.

- **AI's Role:**

o Aggregated user feedback and identified unmet needs.

o Suggested creative playlist themes and algorithmic adjustments.

o Helped the team prioritize features based on predicted engagement metrics.

- **Outcome:** Spotify launched new playlist tools that boosted user satisfaction and engagement rates.

7. Canva: Streamlining Product Updates with AI

The graphic design platform Canva uses AI to align global teams during product ideation and updates.

- **Scenario:** Canva's design and engineering teams collaborated to enhance user templates for specific industries.

- **AI's Role:**

o Analyzed trends in user preferences across regions.

o Suggested design elements, such as colors and layouts, tailored to industry demands.

- o Created predictive models to evaluate potential user adoption of new features.

- **Outcome:** The streamlined approach led to faster implementation of popular templates, improving user retention and market competitiveness.

Key Takeaways from Real-World Examples

- **AI Enhances Inclusivity:** By analyzing diverse inputs, AI ensures that every voice is heard and valued, fostering a more inclusive collaborative environment.

- **Efficiency Gains:** AI accelerates the alignment process by categorizing ideas, highlighting connections, and resolving conflicts.

- **Data-Driven Insights:** AI empowers teams to make informed decisions by integrating real-time analytics and predictive modeling into the brainstorming process.

- **Human-AI Collaboration:** Success relies on blending AI's analytical strengths with human intuition, creativity, and judgment.

Interactive Exercise: Running Your First AI-Enhanced Brainstorm

This exercise is designed to help teams incorporate AI into their brainstorming sessions effectively. By following the steps below, you'll learn how to use AI tools to generate, refine, and align creative ideas while ensuring collaboration and engagement among team members.

Objective

Use AI to facilitate a brainstorming session, generating actionable ideas and aligning diverse inputs into a cohesive plan.

Preparation

1. **Define the Goal:**
   Determine the specific focus of your brainstorming session (e.g., product innovation, marketing strategies, or customer engagement).

   o Example Goal: Generate ideas for a new product feature that enhances user engagement.

2. **Choose an AI Tool:**
   Select an AI-powered collaboration or brainstorming tool such as ChatGPT, Miro AI, or Jasper. Ensure all team members are familiar with its basic functionalities.

3. **Set the Agenda:**
   Outline a structure for the session:

   o **Introduction:** Define the problem or opportunity.

   o **Idea Generation:** Use AI to gather diverse ideas.

   o **Idea Refinement:** Refine and evaluate ideas collaboratively.

   o **Action Plan:** Align and finalize the ideas into an actionable strategy.

4. **Invite Participants:**
   Include a mix of team members from various backgrounds or departments to ensure diverse perspectives.

Step 1: Framing the Challenge

1. **Prompt the AI to Define the Problem:**
   Use a clear and structured question to ensure a focused session.

o   Example Prompt: *"What are some innovative ways to enhance user engagement for a mobile fitness app?"*

2. **Refine the Problem Statement:**

o   Allow the team to review AI-generated insights and add their perspectives.

o   Example Output: AI identifies trends like gamification, community building, and personalized content.

Step 2: Generating Ideas

1. **Start with a Broad Prompt:**
   Encourage AI to propose multiple creative solutions.

o   Example Prompt: *"What features could we introduce to gamify the user experience?"*

2. **Collaborative Idea Building:**

o   Team members contribute their ideas while using AI suggestions for inspiration.

o   AI clusters similar ideas (e.g., leaderboards, reward systems, virtual challenges).

3. **Divergent Thinking Techniques:**
   Ask AI to guide the team in brainstorming unconventional approaches.

o   Example Prompt: *"List 10 out-of-the-box ways to increase app engagement that competitors might not be using."*

Step 3: Refining and Categorizing Ideas

1. **Organize Ideas with AI:**
   Use AI tools to group related suggestions into categories.

o Example Output:

- **Category 1:** Community Features (e.g., social challenges, group leaderboards).

- **Category 2:** Personalization (e.g., tailored workout plans).

- **Category 3:** Gamification (e.g., reward points, badges).

2. **Evaluate Feasibility:**
   Prompt AI to analyze the feasibility and potential impact of each idea.

o Example Prompt: *"Rank these ideas based on ease of implementation and projected user engagement."*

3. **Encourage Feedback:**
   Team members discuss AI rankings and add their insights to refine the list further.

Step 4: Aligning Ideas into a Unified Plan

1. **Prioritize the Top Ideas:**
   Use AI to create a decision matrix for prioritization.

o Example Prompt: *"Help us compare these ideas based on cost, timeline, and expected ROI."*

2. **Visualize the Plan:**

o Use tools like Miro AI or Notion AI to create a visual roadmap.

o   Highlight milestones, resource allocation, and deliverables.

3. **Create an Actionable Summary:**
    Prompt AI to summarize the session into a clear plan.

o   Example Output:

▪   *Top Priority: Launch a gamified rewards system within three months.*

▪   *Next Steps: Assign a team to develop a prototype and test with a focus group.*

Step 5: Post-Session Review

1. **Collect Feedback:**
    Ask participants for their impressions of the AI's contributions and overall session effectiveness.

2. **Iterate for Improvement:**
    Refine your approach to AI-enhanced brainstorming based on feedback.

o   Example Prompt: *"How can we improve the next AI-powered brainstorming session?"*

Key Takeaways

- **AI as a Facilitator:** Treat AI as a tool to enhance—not replace—human creativity.

- **Diverse Perspectives:** Encourage active participation from team members to ensure balanced contributions.

- **Action-Oriented Output:** Use AI to streamline idea refinement and create actionable next steps

Overcoming Mental Blocks with AI

The Nature of Creative Blocks

Creativity is often romanticized as an unending well of inspiration, but even the most innovative minds face moments of stagnation. These creative blocks can feel like hitting an invisible wall—a frustrating inability to think beyond the obvious or muster new ideas. To understand how to overcome these blocks, we must first explore their roots.

Creative blocks arise for various reasons, often rooted in psychological and situational factors. Stress, self-doubt, and perfectionism can cloud the mind, making it difficult to see possibilities. When your brain is preoccupied with fear of failure or external pressures, its capacity to think expansively shrinks. Similarly, burnout and exhaustion strip the mind of its natural curiosity and energy, leaving it in a state of creative inertia.

Beyond the internal causes, situational factors also play a role. A rigid routine or a monotonous environment can stifle imagination. The absence of diverse perspectives or the insistence on staying within predefined boundaries can further exacerbate creative stagnation. When we repeatedly approach challenges the same way, we train our minds to tread familiar paths, making it harder to forge new ones.

Traditional methods for overcoming creative blocks often rely on brainstorming, stepping away from the task, or seeking inspiration through unrelated activities. While effective to a degree, these approaches can lack structure or fail to produce results under time constraints. For example, simply "waiting for inspiration to strike" might not be practical in a high-pressure work environment.

This is where AI enters the picture as a game-changer. Unlike the human mind, which is influenced by emotions, biases, and fatigue, AI processes information systematically and without judgment. It can quickly generate diverse ideas, analyze complex problems, and propose unconventional solutions. By acting as a creative partner, AI helps us bypass psychological and situational barriers, providing a fresh lens through which to view our challenges.

Creative blocks are not insurmountable; they are simply a signal that the mind needs a new approach or perspective. With AI as a tool, we can transform these frustrating moments into opportunities for exploration, collaboration, and innovation. In the sections to come, we will delve into specific ways AI can help us reawaken our creativity, offering strategies and prompts that not only spark ideas but also encourage a deeper understanding of the challenges at hand.

Prompts for Breaking Out of Creative Ruts

When stuck in a creative rut, the key to breaking free is shaking up your thought patterns. AI can be a powerful partner in this process, offering diverse perspectives and sparking unconventional ideas. By crafting intentional prompts, you can guide AI to generate insights that disrupt stale thinking and ignite fresh creativity. Below are approaches to creating effective prompts and examples to inspire you.

1. Encouraging Divergent Thinking

Divergent thinking involves generating multiple ideas or solutions, even if they seem unrelated or far-fetched. AI excels at this by processing vast amounts of information and producing unexpected combinations.

Prompts to Encourage Divergent Thinking:

- *"Generate 10 completely different ways to solve [specific problem]."*

- *"List unusual but plausible applications for [product/idea]."*

- *"Combine [two unrelated concepts] and describe a potential use case."*

Example in Action:

Imagine a team stuck on how to design a new eco-friendly packaging. A prompt like *"Suggest packaging ideas inspired by nature's processes (e.g., photosynthesis, honeycomb structures, animal shells)"* could lead to innovative biomimicry-inspired designs.

2. Challenging Assumptions

Sometimes, the biggest barrier to creativity is unexamined assumptions. AI can help identify and challenge these blind spots, leading to breakthroughs.

Prompts to Challenge Assumptions:

- *"What assumptions am I making about [this situation] that could be incorrect?"*

- *"What would happen if [core assumption] were removed or reversed?"*

- *"Propose a solution to [problem] that ignores traditional constraints."*

Example in Action:

A company might assume its target audience only values low prices. A prompt like *"Suggest marketing strategies that emphasize quality over price for this product"* could open new avenues for premium branding.

3. Generating Contrasting Perspectives

AI can simulate viewpoints from various personas, roles, or disciplines, offering insights you might not have considered.

Prompts for Contrasting Perspectives:

- *"Describe this challenge from the perspective of [a child, competitor, artist, or environmentalist]."*

- *"How would [specific profession, e.g., engineer, historian] approach this problem?"*

- *"Suggest ideas for solving this issue that align with [specific cultural values or practices]."*

Example in Action:

In a team struggling to create an inclusive workplace policy, a prompt like *"Generate suggestions from the perspective of a new employee navigating workplace dynamics"* can highlight overlooked onboarding challenges.

4. Exploring 'What If' Scenarios

'What if' scenarios encourage playful exploration and bold experimentation. AI can imagine alternate realities that spark new possibilities.

Prompts to Explore Scenarios:

- *"What if [this limitation] didn't exist? How would the solution change?"*

- *"Imagine [industry/technology] in 10 years. What innovations would exist?"*

- *"Describe an extreme version of this idea and how it could work."*

Example in Action:

A tech startup unsure about expanding globally could ask, *"What if our product were adapted to thrive in a completely offline environment?"* This could inspire solutions for underserved markets.

5. Injecting Randomness to Spark Ideas

Random associations can lead to serendipitous discoveries. AI can generate surprising inputs to stimulate fresh ideas.

Prompts to Spark Randomness:

- *"Combine [a random object] with [your challenge]. What connections can you draw?"*

- *"Suggest 5 analogies between [your problem] and everyday activities."*

- *"Generate a list of random words or concepts. Use one to inspire a new solution for [specific task]."*

Example in Action:

For a stagnant branding effort, a prompt like *"Combine our product with the concept of space exploration and describe a new tagline"* could lead to an out-of-this-world marketing idea.

6. Crafting Reverse Prompts

Working backward from a goal can illuminate fresh approaches to achieving it.

Reverse Engineering Prompts:

- *"Describe the steps needed to achieve [desired outcome]."*

- *"What would need to change in [current situation] to make [specific goal] inevitable?"*

- *"What are the obstacles to achieving [goal], and how can they be eliminated?"*

Example in Action:

If a team aims to increase customer engagement, they might ask, *"What steps would lead a customer to recommend our product to 10 friends?"* This could reveal overlooked elements of the user experience.

By using these prompts, readers can break out of creative ruts and approach challenges with a renewed sense of curiosity and possibility. In the next section, we'll explore how to use AI to reframe challenges, unlocking even deeper insights into problem-solving and ideation.

Techniques for Reframing Challenges with AI

Reframing is a cognitive tool that shifts how we perceive a problem, helping us see new possibilities where previously there seemed to be none. AI's ability to process vast perspectives and simulate alternative viewpoints makes it an excellent partner in this process. By leveraging AI, we can uncover innovative solutions, challenge ingrained assumptions, and approach challenges from entirely new angles.

1. Shifting the Perspective

Changing the angle from which a problem is viewed can illuminate solutions that were previously obscured. AI can simulate viewpoints from different stakeholders or roles, offering fresh insights.

How to Use AI:

- Ask AI to describe the problem from the perspective of someone directly affected, such as a customer, employee, or competitor.

- Use prompts that frame the challenge in terms of opportunities rather than obstacles.

Example Prompt:

- *"Describe this challenge as if you were [a startup founder, an artist, or an environmentalist]."*

- *"Frame [specific problem] as an opportunity for growth or innovation rather than a limitation."*

Illustration in Action:

A retailer facing declining in-store foot traffic might ask, *"How would a digital-first brand view this issue?"* The AI could propose strategies like experiential in-store events that merge physical and online experiences.

2. Flipping the Problem

Sometimes, inverting a problem can reveal surprising pathways to solutions. This technique focuses on exploring the opposite of the assumed challenge.

How to Use AI:

- Direct AI to imagine the exact opposite of the current issue or goal.

- Ask it to envision what failure looks like and suggest ways to avoid it.

Example Prompt:

- *"What would happen if we aimed for the opposite of our current goal? How could that inform a new approach?"*

- *"Imagine this project failing spectacularly. What mistakes would lead to that outcome, and how can we avoid them?"*

Illustration in Action:

A product team struggling to increase app engagement could ask, *"What features would make users stop using our app altogether?"* This could highlight pain points like intrusive notifications or a cluttered interface that need addressing.

3. Breaking Down the Challenge into Components

Large, abstract challenges can feel insurmountable. By deconstructing them into smaller, manageable parts, AI can help reframe the problem and make solutions more accessible.

How to Use AI:

- Instruct AI to break the problem into specific elements or stages.

- Request insights on each component to uncover overlooked factors.

Example Prompt:

- *"Break down this problem into its core components and suggest solutions for each part."*

- *"Analyze the challenge in terms of [specific aspects, e.g., time, resources, user needs, or logistics]."*

Illustration in Action:

A non-profit facing donor fatigue could prompt AI with, *"What are the main barriers to donor engagement, and how can each be addressed individually?"* Solutions might include simplifying donation processes or crafting emotionally resonant appeals.

4. Reframing Through Analogies and Metaphors

Analogies and metaphors can make a problem relatable and inspire creative approaches by connecting it to familiar concepts.

How to Use AI:

- Ask AI to generate analogies or metaphors that liken the challenge to other systems, ideas, or processes.

- Use the comparison to explore parallels and draw actionable insights.

Example Prompt:

- *"What analogy best describes [specific problem], and how can it inform our approach?"*

- *"Compare this issue to [a natural phenomenon, historical event, or cultural tradition] and suggest lessons we can apply."*

Illustration in Action:

A logistics company grappling with delays could prompt, *"What natural systems (e.g., rivers, beehives) operate efficiently despite challenges, and what can we learn from them?"* This might inspire solutions like decentralized decision-making or flow optimization.

5. Reimagining Constraints as Catalysts

Constraints often feel limiting, but they can also serve as creative catalysts. AI can help turn these constraints into opportunities for innovation.

How to Use AI:

- Frame constraints as design challenges rather than limitations.

- Ask AI to propose solutions that leverage constraints as strengths.

Example Prompt:

- *"How can we turn [specific constraint] into a competitive advantage?"*

- *"Suggest creative solutions that embrace our budget/time/resource limitations."*

Illustration in Action:

A small startup with limited marketing funds could ask, *"What are innovative, low-cost ways to create buzz for our product?"* AI might suggest guerrilla marketing tactics or community-driven campaigns.

6. Scenario Simulation

Exploring "what if" scenarios can uncover hidden dimensions of a challenge and inspire out-of-the-box thinking.

How to Use AI:

- Use AI to simulate scenarios with altered conditions or outcomes.

- Experiment with scenarios that stretch beyond traditional approaches.

Example Prompt:

- *"Imagine this challenge occurring in a completely different industry. How might they solve it?"*

- *"Describe a future scenario where this challenge no longer exists. What changes would have occurred to achieve that?"*

Illustration in Action:

A healthcare provider struggling to improve patient satisfaction could ask, *"How would a luxury hotel address our patients' complaints?"* AI might propose improvements in personalization and comfort.

Reframing challenges with AI allows you to see old problems in new ways, revealing paths to innovation that may have been hidden in plain sight. By combining these techniques with intentional prompts, you can unlock a wealth of creative potential and push the boundaries of your problem-solving abilities.

Sparking Serendipity with AI

Serendipity, the unexpected discovery of valuable insights or solutions, often plays a pivotal role in creativity. While traditional brainstorming relies on chance for such breakthroughs, AI can deliberately simulate serendipitous encounters by introducing randomness, exploring unlikely connections, and offering unconventional perspectives. This section delves into how AI can act as a catalyst for serendipity, enabling users to uncover innovative ideas that might otherwise remain hidden.

1. Introducing Randomness to Generate Novel Ideas

Randomness can disrupt familiar thought patterns, prompting new ways of thinking. AI excels at integrating unexpected variables into problem-solving processes, offering suggestions that might initially seem irrelevant but spark valuable insights upon reflection.

How to Use AI:

- Use prompts that encourage the generation of unrelated or absurd ideas.

- Experiment with randomness by asking for solutions inspired by unrelated fields or concepts.

Example Prompt:

- *"Combine [specific problem] with a random concept, like outer space, ancient civilizations, or modern art. What ideas emerge?"*

- *"Generate three completely unrelated approaches to solving this challenge."*

Illustration in Action:

A city planner working on urban traffic flow might ask AI, *"What solutions could a medieval castle architect offer for modern traffic congestion?"* This could inspire innovative traffic systems resembling drawbridge control or layered pathways.

2. Creating Unlikely Connections Between Concepts

The ability to link seemingly unrelated ideas is a hallmark of creative genius. AI can bridge concepts across disciplines, industries, or eras, offering fresh perspectives that transform how challenges are viewed and addressed.

How to Use AI:

- Request AI to draw parallels between the challenge and unrelated domains.

- Ask it to merge elements from different contexts into a cohesive idea.

Example Prompt:

- *"How might [a challenge in healthcare] be approached using strategies from the gaming industry?"*

- *"Combine elements of [specific concept] and [another unrelated field] to address this issue."*

Illustration in Action:

A team designing a more engaging educational platform might ask, *"How would a theme park designer structure an online learning environment?"* This could inspire gamified content delivery and interactive experiences.

3. Simulating Opposing Viewpoints

Encountering divergent perspectives can lead to new insights. AI can simulate multiple viewpoints, including those that challenge conventional assumptions or provide counterarguments.

How to Use AI:

- Ask AI to articulate opposing views or challenge widely accepted solutions.

- Request it to explore "devil's advocate" scenarios to test the resilience of ideas.

Example Prompt:

- *"What would someone with a completely opposite goal propose for this issue?"*

- *"Challenge our current solution by proposing three opposing arguments."*

Illustration in Action:

A sustainability initiative team might ask AI, *"What would someone skeptical of green energy suggest to improve energy systems?"* The resulting insights could uncover overlooked efficiencies or alternative energy sources.

4. Exploring Hypothetical Futures

Serendipity can emerge from imagining how a problem might evolve under different conditions. AI's capacity for scenario planning and speculative thinking allows users to envision future possibilities and draw actionable insights.

How to Use AI:

- Instruct AI to simulate a future where the challenge has already been solved.

- Ask for hypothetical scenarios that radically shift the current context.

Example Prompt:

- *"Imagine this challenge in a world where [specific technology or social trend] dominates. How would it be addressed?"*

- *"Describe a future where this issue no longer exists. What innovations led to that outcome?"*

Illustration in Action:

A retail company exploring sustainability might prompt AI with, *"What would a zero-waste retail model look like in 2050?"* AI could suggest concepts like reusable packaging as a standard or advanced recycling systems embedded in stores.

5. Leveraging Creative Juxtaposition

Juxtaposing contrasting elements can spark unique ideas. By intentionally combining disparate concepts, AI can generate thought-provoking approaches that inspire innovation.

How to Use AI:

- Use prompts that force the blending of opposing or unrelated ideas.

- Request AI to create solutions by merging unexpected elements.

Example Prompt:

- *"What would happen if [a luxury brand] and [a non-profit organization] collaborated on this problem?"*

- *"Combine the aesthetic principles of modern art with the functionality of industrial design to solve this challenge."*

Illustration in Action:

A designer creating affordable housing might ask, *"How could the principles of minimalist art influence low-cost housing construction?"* AI could suggest modular homes with clean, functional designs.

6. Facilitating Iterative "What If" Scenarios

Serendipity thrives in exploratory "what if" questions that invite imaginative possibilities. AI can help users quickly iterate and refine these scenarios.

How to Use AI:

- Ask AI to generate variations of a concept by tweaking one element at a time.

- Experiment with exaggerated or extreme "what if" scenarios.

Example Prompt:

- *"What if we doubled our budget but halved our time? How would we approach this challenge?"*

- *"Imagine solving this problem in a world where gravity doesn't exist. What insights arise?"*

Illustration in Action:

A tech company designing wearable devices might ask AI, *"What if users could only interact with this device using voice commands?"* This could inspire innovative designs for hands-free operation.

By embracing randomness, juxtaposition, and speculative thinking, AI can replicate the serendipitous sparks of creativity that fuel groundbreaking ideas. These techniques not only encourage exploration but also provide a structured way to harness unpredictability, ensuring that serendipity becomes a consistent part of the creative process.

AI as a Partner for Creative Resilience

Resilience is the ability to persist in the face of setbacks, adapt to new challenges, and find opportunities for growth. In the context of creativity, resilience involves overcoming doubts, failures, and stagnation to keep generating new ideas and solving problems. AI can serve as a powerful partner in building and sustaining creative resilience, offering tools and strategies to help individuals and teams navigate obstacles, recover from setbacks, and maintain momentum.

1. Offering Consistent Support During Creative Lulls

Creativity often involves periods of uncertainty or stagnation, where ideas feel elusive. AI, with its capacity for generating endless suggestions and perspectives, can act as a consistent source of inspiration during these moments.

How AI Helps:

- Provides a steady stream of ideas, reducing the pressure to "force" creativity.

- Encourages experimentation by offering suggestions without judgment.

Example Prompt:

- *"Generate 10 new angles for approaching this problem, prioritizing novelty over practicality."*

- *"Offer three surprising analogies for [specific challenge] that could inspire a fresh approach."*

Illustration in Action:

A screenwriter facing writer's block might ask AI, *"What are some unconventional settings for a story about redemption?"* AI could suggest settings like a bustling airport, a remote monastery, or a dystopian underwater city, rekindling their imagination.

2. Helping Reframe Failures as Opportunities

Failures and setbacks can stifle creativity if perceived as insurmountable. AI can assist in reframing these moments by analyzing what went wrong, identifying lessons learned, and generating new ways forward.

How AI Helps:

- Offers alternative interpretations of setbacks to uncover hidden opportunities.

- Suggests iterative improvements to failed ideas or projects.

Example Prompt:

- *"Analyze the weaknesses of [specific failed idea] and propose three ways to improve it."*

- *"What opportunities could arise from the failure of [specific project or goal]?"*

Illustration in Action:

A marketing team might reflect on a failed campaign by asking AI, *"What could this campaign have achieved if it had targeted a different audience or platform?"* AI could suggest pivoting to a niche demographic or exploring interactive digital content.

3. Sustaining Momentum Through Incremental Progress

Building creative resilience often involves celebrating small wins and maintaining progress, even when breakthroughs seem distant. AI can aid in sustaining momentum by facilitating incremental improvements and offering encouragement.

How AI Helps:

- Breaks down large creative tasks into manageable steps.

- Offers quick feedback on partial ideas, enabling continuous refinement.

Example Prompt:

- *"Suggest the next three small steps to develop this concept further."*

- *"Provide constructive feedback on this draft idea and suggest minor adjustments."*

Illustration in Action:

A product development team refining a prototype could use AI to prompt, *"Identify three small design tweaks that could enhance usability."* The resulting suggestions could provide clear, actionable steps to keep the project moving forward.

4. Building Confidence Through Practice and Iteration

Creative resilience grows through practice and the willingness to try again. AI can act as a low-stakes collaborator, allowing individuals to experiment, fail, and refine ideas without fear of judgment or wasted effort.

How AI Helps:

- Creates a safe space for trial and error by offering feedback and alternative ideas.

- Encourages exploration by presenting diverse approaches to a single challenge.

Example Prompt:

- *"Generate three wildly different versions of this idea and explain the unique strengths of each."*

- *"How can this concept be adapted for a completely different audience or use case?"*

Illustration in Action:

A visual artist exploring new styles might ask AI, *"How could I reinterpret this piece using techniques from surrealism, minimalism, and pop art?"* This exercise could inspire fresh creative directions while reinforcing their adaptability.

5. Encouraging Long-Term Vision and Perspective

Creative resilience isn't just about overcoming short-term challenges; it's also about maintaining focus on long-term goals and staying motivated despite obstacles. AI can assist by providing reminders of the bigger picture and generating strategies to align short-term efforts with overarching objectives.

How AI Helps:

- Provides clarity by connecting current challenges to long-term goals.

- Suggests ways to measure progress and celebrate milestones.

Example Prompt:

- *"What are three ways this short-term setback might contribute to achieving our larger vision?"*

- *"Propose a roadmap for turning this concept into a long-term project with measurable milestones."*

Illustration in Action:

An entrepreneur facing funding challenges might ask AI, *"How can this financial setback lead to a stronger, more sustainable business model?"* AI could suggest focusing on lean operations, leveraging partnerships, or exploring alternative revenue streams.

By positioning AI as a collaborative partner, individuals and teams can build creative resilience that endures beyond fleeting inspiration. Whether by reframing failures, sustaining momentum, or encouraging long-term thinking, AI becomes a vital ally in navigating the inevitable ups and downs of the creative process. This partnership not only helps creators overcome obstacles but also empowers them to emerge stronger, more innovative, and more confident in their abilities.

Testing and Refining Ideas with AI

Why Refinement Matters

Every groundbreaking idea starts as a spark of creativity—a rough concept with potential waiting to be realized. However, raw ideas, no matter how brilliant, are rarely ready to implement. Without refinement, even the most promising concepts can fail due to overlooked details, unanticipated risks, or impractical strategies. This is where refinement becomes essential, turning a vague notion into a well-structured, actionable plan.

The Value of Refinement

Refinement is not about tearing ideas apart; it's about strengthening them. It allows us to:

1. **Evaluate Feasibility:** Can this idea be executed with the available resources, within the given timeline, and in alignment with organizational goals?

2. **Mitigate Risks:** Are there potential pitfalls—financial, operational, or market-related—that could derail the plan?

3. **Ensure Scalability:** Can this idea grow and adapt to meet future demands, or will it hit a ceiling too quickly?

Refinement adds depth, focus, and clarity, ensuring that an idea is not just creative but also practical and impactful.

The Challenges of Refinement

Refining ideas is not always easy. People often:

- Overlook critical flaws in their excitement to implement the idea.

- Struggle to identify gaps or risks, especially in complex projects.

- Lack the tools or perspective to assess feasibility and scalability.

Traditional brainstorming sessions often fall short during the refinement phase because they rely heavily on intuition and subjective judgment. This is where AI steps in as a game-changer.

AI as Your Partner in Refinement

Artificial intelligence excels at processing large amounts of information, identifying patterns, and offering data-driven insights. It provides a unique advantage in refining ideas because it can:

- Offer objective feedback, free from bias or emotional attachment.

- Simulate scenarios to predict outcomes and identify risks.

- Suggest solutions, modifications, and optimizations that might not be immediately obvious to humans.

For example, an AI tool can take a rough product concept and help you identify production bottlenecks, refine target demographics, or propose strategies for scaling the product across global markets.

The Purpose of This Chapter

This chapter will empower you to use AI as a critical tool in the refinement process. You'll learn how to:

1. Write prompts to evaluate the feasibility of your ideas.

2. Use AI to identify risks and propose mitigation strategies.

3. Ensure scalability by leveraging AI's ability to analyze trends and predict growth potential.

4. Transform rough concepts into actionable plans with specific steps and deliverables.

By the end of this chapter, you'll see refinement not as a chore but as a creative superpower. With AI as your partner, you'll be equipped to unlock the full potential of your ideas and turn them into strategies ready to succeed in the real world.

Writing Prompts to Assess Feasibility

Turning an idea into reality requires assessing whether it's practical, achievable, and aligned with your available resources. Feasibility analysis is about asking the right questions, and AI can help provide answers that go beyond surface-level considerations. By crafting well-structured prompts, you can harness AI to evaluate an idea's feasibility from multiple angles, including resource allocation, time management, and organizational fit.

1. What Feasibility Means

Feasibility focuses on whether an idea is capable of being executed successfully within real-world constraints. Key dimensions of feasibility include:

- **Resource Requirements:** Does the idea require specific tools, personnel, or budget allocations?

- **Time Constraints:** Can it be implemented within a defined timeline?

- **Alignment with Goals:** Does the idea align with organizational or strategic objectives?

AI can assist by analyzing these dimensions systematically, uncovering gaps, and offering actionable insights.

2. Crafting Effective Prompts for Feasibility Analysis

The key to effective feasibility prompts is specificity. A vague prompt will yield vague responses. To ensure clarity, your prompts should:

- Clearly define the context of the idea (e.g., its purpose, scope, and intended outcomes).

- Include constraints like budget, timeline, or specific resource limits.

- Request actionable outputs, such as risk factors or recommendations.

3. Prompt Templates for Feasibility Analysis

Basic Feasibility Assessment

1. *"Analyze whether the following idea is feasible within a $[X] budget and a [Y]-month timeline. Highlight any potential barriers or resource constraints."*

2. *"Evaluate the practicality of implementing this idea. What are the key steps needed, and are there any obvious challenges?"*

Resource Requirements

3. *"What resources (e.g., tools, personnel, budget) would be required to execute this idea? Are these resources readily available or difficult to obtain?"*

4. *"Break down the human and material resources needed for this idea and assess if they align with current capacities."*

Timeline Feasibility

5. *"Can this idea be executed within [Z] weeks/months? If not, what adjustments are necessary to meet the timeline?"*

6. *"Provide a timeline of key milestones and deliverables for implementing this idea successfully."*

Organizational Fit

7. *"Does this idea align with the organization's strategic goals? If not, suggest ways to adjust it for better alignment."*

8. *"Assess how this idea fits into the organization's current priorities and whether it overlaps with or conflicts with ongoing initiatives."*

Scenario-Based Feasibility

9. *"Simulate a scenario where this idea is implemented in [specific context]. Identify any challenges that might arise and propose solutions."*

10. *"Compare this idea to a similar project or case study. What lessons can be learned, and how do they apply to this situation?"*

4. Example: Applying Feasibility Prompts

Scenario: You're developing a mobile app to help users track their carbon footprint.

Prompt:

- *"Analyze the feasibility of developing a carbon footprint tracking app with a $100,000 budget and a 6-month timeline. Consider technical requirements, development team size, and   user   acquisition   strategies."*

AI Response (Example):

- Potential Barriers: Difficulty finding a skilled development team within budget, limited timeline for app testing and iteration.

- Recommendations: Focus on a minimal viable product (MVP) for initial launch, outsource specific development tasks to save costs, and allocate 10% of the budget for user testing.

5. Key Tips for Writing Feasibility Prompts

- **Be Specific:** Include clear parameters for budget, time, and resources.

- **Focus on Action:** Request step-by-step recommendations or specific analyses.

- **Iterate:** Refine your prompts based on AI's initial feedback to get more targeted insights.

By using well-crafted prompts, you can make informed decisions about which ideas are worth pursuing and what adjustments they need to succeed.

Identifying and Mitigating Risks with AI

Risk is an inevitable part of any innovative process. Whether you're developing a new product, launching a campaign, or implementing a strategy, unforeseen challenges can emerge at every stage. Identifying risks early and creating mitigation strategies are critical steps in ensuring the success of any idea. AI offers unique capabilities in this area by analyzing data, predicting potential pitfalls, and suggesting proactive solutions.

1. The Importance of Risk Analysis

Risk analysis allows you to:

- **Anticipate Problems:** Spot potential challenges before they escalate.

- **Develop Contingencies:** Create backup plans to address potential setbacks.

- **Optimize Success:** Minimize disruptions and maximize the chances of achieving your goals.

Traditional brainstorming often overlooks certain risks due to cognitive biases, incomplete information, or time constraints. AI's ability to process vast amounts of data and evaluate multiple scenarios makes it a valuable partner in comprehensive risk analysis.

2. How AI Enhances Risk Identification and Mitigation

AI tools excel at identifying risks by:

- **Analyzing Historical Data:** Drawing insights from past projects or industry trends to highlight common pitfalls.

- **Simulating Scenarios:** Running hypothetical models to identify vulnerabilities in your idea.

- **Suggesting Mitigation Strategies:** Offering evidence-based recommendations to address identified risks.

  For example, AI could analyze customer feedback on a similar product to pinpoint design flaws or suggest alternative manufacturing methods to reduce costs.

3. Writing Effective Risk Analysis Prompts

To leverage AI for risk analysis, your prompts should be specific and comprehensive. Ensure your prompts:

- Include the full context of your idea or project.

- Focus on key areas where risks are most likely to occur (e.g., budget, operations, customer adoption).

- Request actionable outputs, such as risk rankings or mitigation strategies.

4. Prompt Templates for Risk Identification and Mitigation

Basic Risk Identification

1. *"Identify the top five risks associated with the following idea. Include financial, operational, and market-related risks."*

2. *"List potential challenges this project might face during development and implementation."*

Scenario-Based Risk Analysis

3. *"Simulate a scenario where this idea is implemented. What challenges might arise, and how can they be addressed?"*

4. *"What are the risks of launching this product in [specific market or industry]? Include cultural, legal, and competitive factors."*

Operational Risks

5. *"Analyze the operational risks of this idea. What supply chain or resource-related issues could arise, and how can they be mitigated?"*

6. *"Identify potential bottlenecks in executing this idea and propose solutions to avoid them."*

Customer and Market Risks

7. *"What are the risks of low customer adoption for this idea? Suggest strategies to improve engagement and acceptance."*

8. *"Evaluate the competitive risks of introducing this product. How can the idea be differentiated to minimize these risks?"*

Mitigation Strategies

9. *"For the following risks, propose specific mitigation strategies and contingency plans: [list risks]."*

10. *"If [specific risk] occurs, what steps should be taken to minimize its impact on the project?"*

5. Example: Applying Risk Analysis Prompts

Scenario: You're planning to launch a subscription-based meal delivery service.

Prompt:

- *"Identify the risks of launching a subscription-based meal delivery service in an urban market. Include risks related to supply chain, customer acquisition, and competitor response. Suggest mitigation strategies for each risk."*

AI Response (Example):

- **Risk 1:** Supply chain disruptions due to ingredient shortages.

o *Mitigation:* Partner with multiple suppliers to ensure redundancy; invest in inventory management software.

- **Risk 2:** High customer acquisition costs.

o *Mitigation:* Launch referral programs and offer discounts for early adopters.

- **Risk 3:** Aggressive competitor pricing.

o *Mitigation:* Differentiate the service by offering unique meal options (e.g., locally sourced, customizable plans).

6. Tips for Effective Risk Mitigation with AI

- **Start Broad, Then Narrow:** Begin with general risk prompts and refine them to focus on specific areas as needed.

- **Iterate on Responses:** Use AI feedback to generate follow-up prompts for deeper insights.

- **Combine Human Judgment:** AI can identify and suggest risks, but human expertise is essential for evaluating recommendations in context.

By integrating AI into your risk analysis process, you can approach challenges with greater confidence, anticipate obstacles, and proactively develop solutions that keep your ideas on track.

Evaluating Scalability with AI

Scalability is the capacity of an idea, product, or process to grow and adapt as demand increases without sacrificing quality or efficiency. Whether you're launching a new business, implementing a solution, or refining a concept, evaluating scalability is a crucial step in ensuring long-term success. AI can play a significant role in this evaluation by analyzing data, forecasting growth scenarios, and offering actionable insights for scaling effectively.

1. Why Scalability Matters

An idea that works well on a small scale might encounter challenges when expanded. Assessing scalability allows you to:

- **Plan for Growth:** Understand the resources, infrastructure, and systems required to scale effectively.

- **Avoid Overextension:** Identify bottlenecks or inefficiencies that could arise as operations grow.

- **Optimize Investment:** Allocate resources where they will have the most impact during scaling.

Scalability is especially critical in fast-moving industries where the ability to scale quickly can mean the difference between success and failure.

2. How AI Enhances Scalability Analysis

AI provides a data-driven approach to evaluating scalability by:

- **Simulating Growth Scenarios:** Analyzing how your idea performs under varying levels of demand or operational complexity.

- **Identifying Scaling Challenges:** Highlighting potential bottlenecks in supply chains, staffing, or technology.

- **Optimizing Resource Allocation:** Suggesting efficient ways to scale infrastructure, processes, or customer acquisition strategies.

3. Writing Effective Prompts for Scalability Analysis

To use AI for scalability evaluation, your prompts should:

- **Define the Context:** Clearly describe the current state of your idea or operation.

- **Focus on Growth Factors:** Specify areas where scalability is a concern, such as operations, finances, or market penetration.

- **Request Specific Outputs:** Ask for recommendations, potential risks, or step-by-step scaling strategies.

4. Prompt Templates for Scalability Evaluation

General Scalability Analysis

1. *"Analyze the scalability of the following idea: [insert description]. Identify potential challenges and suggest improvements."*

2. *"What factors could limit the scalability of this product or service? Provide recommendations to address these limitations."*

Operational Scalability

3. *"Evaluate how the following operations can scale to meet increasing demand. Identify potential bottlenecks and propose solutions."*

4. *"What resources or systems are required to scale this process from [current scale] to [target scale]?"*

Financial Scalability

5. *"Analyze the financial scalability of this business model. What challenges might arise, and how can they be mitigated?"*

6. *"If revenue increases by [percentage], how should costs and investments adjust to maintain profitability?"*

Technical Scalability

7. *"Evaluate the technical scalability of this system. Will it handle a 10x increase in usage? If not, what changes are required?"*

8. *"What improvements can be made to ensure that this software or platform scales effectively with user growth?"*

Market Scalability

9. *"How can this product or service scale to reach a broader audience? Suggest strategies for expanding market penetration."*

10. *"Identify potential market segments for scaling this idea and recommend approaches to reach them effectively."*

5. Example: Applying Scalability Prompts

Scenario: You're developing a subscription-based learning platform for small businesses.

Prompt:

- *"Evaluate the scalability of a subscription-based learning platform for small businesses. Identify potential operational, financial, and technical challenges and recommend solutions."*

AI Response (Example):

- **Operational Challenges:** Limited course creation capacity as demand grows.

o *Solution:* Automate course content updates and explore partnerships with industry experts for scalable content development.

- **Financial Challenges:** High customer acquisition costs in new markets.

o *Solution:* Use AI-driven marketing tools to identify cost-effective channels for acquiring customers.

- **Technical Challenges:** Increased platform usage leading to slower performance.

o *Solution:* Transition to cloud-based infrastructure for scalable performance.

6. Best Practices for Scalability Analysis

- **Run Multiple Scenarios:** Use AI to simulate different scaling scenarios, such as rapid growth or gradual expansion.

- **Iterate on Feedback:** Refine AI-generated insights by posing follow-up prompts for deeper analysis.

- **Integrate Human Oversight:** Combine AI's scalability predictions with insights from stakeholders and industry experts to ensure practicality.

By leveraging AI to evaluate scalability, you can anticipate growth challenges, optimize processes, and confidently expand your operations or ideas without compromising on quality or efficiency.

Refining Rough Ideas into Actionable Strategies

Transforming a raw idea into a concrete, actionable strategy is a critical step in the creative process. While initial brainstorming might generate a flood of concepts, refining these ideas ensures they are clear, practical, and implementable. AI serves as an invaluable partner in this process, offering structure, clarity, and strategic insights that can turn vague notions into viable solutions.

1. Why Refinement is Key

Refinement bridges the gap between creativity and execution. A rough idea might be exciting, but without refinement, it risks being impractical or incomplete. Key benefits of refinement include:

- **Clarity:** Breaking down abstract concepts into specific, actionable steps.

- **Feasibility:** Ensuring ideas can be realistically implemented within given constraints.

- **Alignment:** Tailoring ideas to align with goals, resources, and stakeholder needs.

2. The Role of AI in Refining Ideas

AI excels at taking broad or ambiguous inputs and generating structured, actionable outputs. It can:

- **Clarify Objectives:** Help you define the core purpose and goals of your idea.

- **Develop Strategies:** Suggest step-by-step plans for implementation.

- **Highlight Gaps:** Identify missing elements or areas needing further exploration.

- **Validate Assumptions:** Test the idea's logic and provide constructive feedback.

3. Writing Prompts for Idea Refinement

Effective prompts for refining rough ideas focus on breaking down the concept, exploring its components, and building a pathway to action.

Prompt Structure:

1. **Start with Context:** Provide a brief description of the rough idea.

2. **Focus on Goals:** Specify what you want the AI to refine (e.g., steps, challenges, key metrics).

3. **Request Actionable Outputs:** Ask for a clear strategy, roadmap, or checklist.

4. Prompt Templates for Refining Ideas

General Refinement Prompts

1. *"Refine the following idea: [insert idea]. Provide a step-by-step strategy for implementation."*

2. *"What steps can be taken to transform this idea into a viable business plan?"*

Focus on Specific Goals

3. *"Identify the key objectives and necessary resources for implementing this idea: [insert idea]."*

4. *"Break down this idea into actionable steps that can be executed within [timeframe or budget]."*

Exploring Feasibility

5. *"Evaluate the practicality of this idea. What adjustments would make it more feasible?"*

6. *"Identify potential obstacles in implementing this idea and suggest ways to overcome them."*

Clarifying Details

7. *"Expand on this idea by providing detailed strategies for [specific aspect]."*

8. *"What are the key metrics to measure success for this idea? How can they be tracked?"*

5. Example: Refining a Rough Idea

Scenario: You have a rough idea for a subscription service that delivers eco-friendly office supplies.

Prompt:

- *"Refine this idea: A subscription service for eco-friendly office supplies. Provide a detailed strategy, including product offerings, target audience, pricing, and marketing plan."*

AI Response (Example):

1. **Product Offerings:**

- Curate monthly boxes with eco-friendly essentials (e.g., recycled paper, biodegradable pens).

- Offer tiered subscription plans based on company size.

2. **Target Audience:**

- Small to mid-sized businesses with sustainability goals.

- Freelancers and remote workers committed to eco-friendly practices.

3. **Pricing Strategy:**

- Tiered pricing: Basic ($20/month), Standard ($50/month), Premium ($100/month).

4. **Marketing Plan:**

- Leverage social media to showcase eco-friendly tips.

- Partner with environmental organizations for co-branded campaigns.

- Use AI to analyze audience engagement and optimize marketing messages.

6. Best Practices for Refining Ideas with AI

1. **Iterate Frequently:** Use multiple prompts to refine different aspects of the idea (e.g., feasibility, risks, audience targeting).

2. **Request Alternatives:** Ask AI to suggest alternative strategies or approaches to keep options open.

3. **Focus on Outcomes:** Ensure refinement efforts are tied to clear goals, such as solving a problem, meeting a need, or achieving a specific impact.

4. **Collaborate with Humans:** Combine AI insights with team feedback to balance creativity and practicality.

Refining rough ideas into actionable strategies ensures they move from potential to reality. By leveraging AI to streamline this process, you can enhance clarity, uncover opportunities, and create impactful solutions tailored to your goals.

Interactive Exercises and Case Studies

Interactive exercises and real-world case studies help readers apply concepts, practice refining ideas, and understand how AI can streamline the process. Below is a structured approach to incorporate both into this section.

1. Interactive Exercises

Exercise 1: Breaking Down the Idea
Objective: Teach readers how to dissect a rough idea into actionable components.
Steps:

1. Write down a rough idea (e.g., "A mobile app for personalized fitness plans").

2. Break it into components:

o Core purpose: What is the main goal of this app?

o Target audience: Who benefits from this app?

o Features: What makes it unique or valuable?

o   Challenges: What might hinder its success?

3.   Use the following prompt to refine:

o   *"Refine this idea: [insert idea]. Break it into actionable components, including purpose, target audience, features, and challenges."*

4.   Compare the AI's response with your initial breakdown and refine further.

Exercise 2: Writing an Effective Prompt

Objective: Help readers practice crafting strong prompts.

Steps:

1.   Choose a rough idea or use this example: *"A subscription box for gourmet coffee lovers."*

2.   Write a general prompt: *"Refine this idea."*

3.   Write a detailed prompt: *"Refine this idea into an actionable business strategy, including target audience, pricing, marketing plan, and potential challenges."*

4.   Input both prompts into an AI tool and compare results.

o   Discuss how specificity improves the output and brainstorm ways to make prompts even more effective.

Exercise 3: Evaluating Feasibility and Scalability

Objective: Practice using AI to assess ideas.

Steps:

1.   Take an idea like *"An eco-friendly delivery service using e-bikes in urban areas."*

2.   Craft prompts to assess:

o   Feasibility: *"What are the key factors that determine the feasibility of this idea?"*

o   Scalability: *"How can this idea scale to multiple cities while maintaining cost efficiency?"*

3.   Analyze AI's responses and list practical steps for implementation.

4.   Reflect: Which parts of the idea were strengthened, and which require more thought?

2. Case Studies

Case Study 1: Refining a Social Enterprise Idea
Scenario: A team wants to create a nonprofit organization that provides free coding workshops for underprivileged youth.
Steps Taken:

1.   Initial Idea: *"Offer free coding workshops to underprivileged youth."*

2.   Refinement Prompt:

o   *"Refine this idea into a structured program, including target demographics, curriculum design, funding sources, and scalability options."*

3.   AI-Generated Output:

o   Target Demographics: Youth aged 10–18 in low-income communities.

o   Curriculum: Beginner-friendly coding languages (e.g., Python, HTML) with a project-based approach.

o   Funding: Corporate sponsorships, grant applications, and crowdfunding campaigns.

o   Scalability: Partner with schools and libraries to expand reach.

Outcome: The team implemented the refined strategy, secured funding, and expanded to three cities within a year.

Case Study 2: Revamping a Marketing Strategy

Scenario: A small business wants to increase awareness of its handmade jewelry brand.

Steps Taken:

1. Initial Idea: *"Launch a social media marketing campaign."*

2. Refinement Prompt:

o *"Develop a detailed social media marketing strategy for this handmade jewelry brand, targeting young professionals."*

3. AI-Generated Output:

o Platforms: Focus on Instagram and Pinterest.

o Content Ideas: Highlight craftsmanship through behind-the-scenes videos, customer testimonials, and influencer partnerships.

o Schedule: Post 4–5 times weekly, with themed days (e.g., #MakerMonday, #StylingTips).

o Metrics: Track engagement rates, website clicks, and conversion rates.

Outcome: The business saw a 40% increase in engagement and a 25% boost in sales over three months.

3. Best Practices for Exercises and Case Studies

• **Interactive Exercises:** Ensure exercises are simple to follow, with clear instructions and examples. Encourage readers to share results in group settings or online forums for feedback.

- **Case Studies:** Use diverse industries (e.g., tech, nonprofit, retail) to demonstrate versatility. Include before-and-after comparisons to show how AI refinement made a difference.

Refinement as a Creative Superpower

Refinement isn't just about polishing rough edges; it's about transforming good ideas into extraordinary ones. In this section, we'll explore how refinement becomes a superpower, empowering innovators to navigate complexity, unlock hidden potential, and craft solutions that stand out. AI is the catalyst that makes this process faster, more effective, and accessible to everyone.

1. The Power of Iteration

Refinement is iterative. It's the process of revisiting and reshaping an idea until it reaches its fullest potential. Creative refinement involves:

- **Expanding possibilities:** Thinking beyond the first idea to uncover new angles.

- **Distilling clarity:** Removing excess and focusing on the core message or value.

- **Testing assumptions:** Exploring what works and why, then making adjustments.

Example: Think of an inventor designing a product. The first prototype may only partially solve a problem. Through refinement, the design evolves to be more efficient, user-friendly, and marketable.

With AI: The iterative cycle is supercharged. You can test dozens of variations in minutes, allowing you to focus on evaluating and improving outcomes.

2. AI as a Creative Amplifier

AI enhances refinement by acting as a partner in the creative process. While humans provide the vision, AI offers the tools to refine that vision. This collaboration transforms the refinement process in several ways:

- **Speed:** AI can generate and evaluate ideas in seconds, saving hours of brainstorming.

- **Perspective:** It introduces viewpoints or insights that might not occur to a human team.

- **Detail:** It helps users break down abstract ideas into actionable steps.

Example Prompt:
"Refine the idea for a digital platform that connects freelance artists with businesses. Break it into core features, a pricing model, and a marketing plan tailored to startups."

3. Refinement vs. Perfection

It's important to recognize that refinement isn't about perfection—it's about progress. Chasing perfection can stifle creativity, while focusing on refinement encourages exploration and flexibility.

- **Refinement encourages action:** Start with what you have and improve iteratively.

- **Perfection discourages innovation:** It delays action due to fear of imperfection.

AI assists in this balance by providing quick feedback loops, enabling continuous improvement without paralysis.

4. Practical Benefits of Refinement as a Superpower

- **Problem-solving clarity:** Refinement helps untangle complex challenges by breaking them into manageable parts.

- **Adaptability:** Ideas become flexible enough to meet changing needs or circumstances.

- **Confidence:** A well-refined idea instills confidence in stakeholders, making it easier to gain support or investment.

Real-World Example:
Consider the launch of Tesla's electric cars. The initial models focused on performance and sustainability. Through refinement, Tesla expanded its focus to include luxury design, advanced technology (like autopilot), and an accessible charging network. This multi-faceted approach turned an innovative concept into an industry disruptor.

5. Embracing Refinement with AI

AI makes refinement a superpower for everyone, not just seasoned professionals. By providing instant feedback, offering alternative perspectives, and helping refine the smallest details, AI enables individuals to create solutions that are sharper, more innovative, and more impactful.

Call to Action:

Refinement is no longer a skill reserved for elite creators or extensive resources. With AI, anyone can elevate their creative potential and unlock the full power of their ideas. Embrace refinement, and let it transform your approach to innovation.

Part 4: Ethical and Practical Considerations

Avoiding Over-Reliance on AI

AI has transformed how we approach problem-solving and creativity, offering speed, scalability, and an endless stream of possibilities. However, it is essential to understand where its capabilities fall short to harness its potential effectively while avoiding pitfalls. Below, we delve into the core limitations of AI in creativity and why human involvement remains irreplaceable.

1. Mechanical Creativity vs. Human Creativity

AI generates ideas through algorithms trained on vast datasets. While this enables it to mimic creativity, its process is inherently mechanical.

- **Lack of Original Thought**: AI cannot produce ideas entirely disconnected from its training data. Its "creativity" is a synthesis of preexisting information, often leading to derivative rather than groundbreaking concepts.

- **Absence of Emotional Resonance**: Creativity often stems from human emotions, experiences, and intuition—qualities that AI lacks. This can result in outputs that feel cold, impersonal, or out of touch with emotional or cultural contexts.

Example: An AI might suggest a visually striking advertisement, but without human input, it might miss the emotional nuance needed to resonate with a specific audience.

2. Contextual Blind Spots

AI struggles with understanding context beyond its programming. This can lead to ideas that are technically accurate but culturally, socially, or ethically inappropriate.

- **Misinterpreting Cultural Nuances**: AI lacks the lived experiences required to grasp cultural subtleties, which can result in tone-deaf suggestions.

- **Failing to Adapt to Specific Situations**: While AI can generate general solutions, it often lacks the flexibility to tailor ideas to niche or highly specific scenarios.

Example: In a brainstorming session for global marketing, AI might propose a slogan that works well in one language but translates poorly— or offensively—into another.

3. Risk of Homogenization

Over-reliance on AI can inadvertently lead to a homogenization of ideas.

- **Repetitive Patterns**: AI's reliance on patterns and trends can result in outputs that feel generic or overly similar to existing solutions.

- **Stifling Divergence**: True creativity often requires challenging conventions and thinking outside the box—an area where AI's algorithmic nature can struggle.

Example: AI might suggest a design trend popular in the industry but fail to propose something unique that sets a brand apart.

4. Ethical and Social Implications

AI-generated ideas can inadvertently reinforce biases present in its training data.

- **Bias Amplification**: If the data used to train AI contains stereotypes or prejudices, these can surface in its creative outputs.

- **Lack of Ethical Judgment**: AI cannot assess the moral or social implications of its suggestions, requiring human oversight to ensure responsible application.

Example: An AI-generated hiring campaign might unintentionally favor certain demographics based on biased training data, leading to discriminatory practices.

Why These Limitations Matter

Recognizing these limitations highlights the importance of human oversight in the creative process. While AI excels at generating ideas quickly and at scale, humans bring emotional intelligence, ethical judgment, and the ability to think beyond data-driven patterns. These qualities are vital for creating solutions that are not only innovative but also impactful, relevant, and meaningful.

Key Insight: AI is a powerful ally in creativity, but it must be paired with human intuition, empathy, and critical thinking to achieve truly remarkable outcomes.

Practical Takeaway

When working with AI in creative processes:

1. Always evaluate AI outputs for emotional and cultural relevance.

2. Be mindful of repetitive or overly conventional suggestions.

3. Use AI as a starting point but rely on human creativity to refine and personalize ideas.

This understanding lays the groundwork for integrating AI into brainstorming while ensuring it complements rather than replaces human creativity.

The Role of Human Oversight in Brainstorming

While AI offers a powerful tool for brainstorming, its potential is fully realized only when paired with human oversight. Humans bring emotional intelligence, contextual understanding, and ethical discernment to the creative process, ensuring that AI-generated ideas are relevant, meaningful, and actionable. This section explores the key ways in which human oversight enhances brainstorming with AI.

1. Adding Emotional and Cultural Context

AI can process vast amounts of data but lacks the ability to understand or feel emotions. Humans play a crucial role in bridging this gap.

- **Emotional Resonance**: Creativity often requires tapping into emotions to connect with audiences. Humans interpret AI-generated ideas through the lens of emotional and cultural significance, refining them to create meaningful impact.

- **Cultural Sensitivity**: Humans understand cultural nuances that AI cannot, ensuring that ideas align with societal norms, values, and expectations.

Example: AI might suggest a bold campaign slogan, but human oversight ensures it evokes the desired emotional response and avoids cultural missteps.

2. Ensuring Relevance and Practicality

AI can generate a wide array of ideas, but not all are practical or applicable. Human oversight ensures that outputs align with specific goals and constraints.

- **Tailoring to Context**: Humans evaluate whether AI-generated ideas are suitable for the particular audience, industry, or problem at hand.

- **Filtering and Refining**: By selecting and improving the best ideas, humans transform raw AI suggestions into actionable solutions.

Example: AI might propose several innovative product features, but humans determine which are feasible within budgetary and technical limitations.

3. Injecting Ethical Judgment

AI lacks the ability to discern right from wrong, which can lead to outputs that are ethically questionable. Humans ensure that brainstorming processes adhere to ethical standards.

- **Addressing Biases**: Humans identify and correct biases in AI-generated ideas, promoting fairness and inclusivity.

- **Assessing Ethical Implications**: Humans consider the broader impact of ideas, avoiding unintended harm or controversy.

  Example: AI might suggest a cost-cutting measure that involves replacing human jobs, but human oversight evaluates the ethical and social implications of such a decision.

4. Fostering Divergent Thinking

AI often operates within the boundaries of its training data, which can limit creativity. Humans push these boundaries by introducing fresh perspectives and challenging conventional thinking.

- **Encouraging Innovation**: Humans combine AI-generated ideas with their own insights, fostering original and unconventional solutions.

- **Challenging Conformity**: Humans recognize when AI outputs are overly repetitive or derivative, ensuring that brainstorming sessions yield unique results.

  Example: AI might generate a list of marketing strategies based on existing trends, but humans introduce novel approaches that disrupt the status quo.

5. Maintaining the Human Element in Creativity

Fundamentally, creativity is a deeply human endeavor, driven by personal experiences, intuition, and a desire to connect with others.

- **Building Human Connections**: Humans ensure that ideas resonate on a personal level, creating solutions that are not only innovative but also relatable.

- **Preserving Originality**: By infusing their own perspectives and experiences, humans ensure that AI-generated ideas retain a distinct human touch.

  Example: A team brainstorming session might use AI to spark initial ideas but rely on human insights to develop a narrative that tells a compelling story.

Practical Strategies for Effective Oversight

1. **Collaborate, Don't Delegate**: Treat AI as a partner rather than a replacement in the brainstorming process.

2. **Ask the Right Questions**: Use prompts to guide AI in generating ideas, then critically evaluate the results.

3. **Iterate and Refine**: Continuously improve AI outputs by incorporating human insights and feedback.

4. **Prioritize Ethical Considerations**: Regularly assess the fairness, inclusivity, and societal impact of AI-generated ideas.

   Human oversight transforms AI from a tool for generating ideas into a catalyst for meaningful innovation. By blending the strengths of AI with human intuition, empathy, and critical thinking, brainstorming processes can achieve outcomes that are both creative and impactful.

Balancing Automation and Intuition

The integration of AI in brainstorming presents a unique challenge: finding the right balance between leveraging automated processes and preserving human intuition. While AI excels at processing information and generating ideas, intuition remains essential for creativity, ethical discernment, and strategic decision-making. This section explores how automation and intuition can complement each other to enhance brainstorming outcomes.

---

1. Recognizing the Strengths of Automation

AI's ability to handle large datasets and generate diverse ideas quickly is unmatched. However, understanding where automation thrives helps define its role in the brainstorming process.

- **Efficiency and Scale**: AI can generate a high volume of ideas, identify patterns, and analyze trends faster than humans.

- **Objective Insights**: By operating without emotional biases, AI provides data-driven perspectives that can challenge assumptions.

- **Creative Diversity**: AI can suggest unconventional ideas by synthesizing information from various domains.

  Example: AI might analyze consumer behavior data to propose innovative product features that humans may overlook.

2. The Power of Human Intuition

Intuition is rooted in experience, empathy, and creativity, offering insights that go beyond data. It ensures that brainstorming processes remain human-centered and adaptable.

- **Understanding Context**: Humans grasp nuances, such as emotional resonance or cultural significance, that AI cannot fully comprehend.

- **Spotting the "Big Idea"**: Intuition allows humans to recognize the most promising concepts among AI-generated outputs.

- **Flexibility and Adaptation**: Humans can pivot strategies based on evolving circumstances, something AI struggles to do without explicit input.

    Example: An experienced marketer might sense that a specific tagline resonates deeply with a target audience, even if AI doesn't prioritize it.

3. Avoiding Over-Reliance on Automation

Over-dependence on AI risks losing the creative spontaneity and ethical judgment that intuition brings. Striking a balance ensures the brainstorming process remains innovative and responsible.

- **Quality Over Quantity**: AI can flood users with ideas, but humans filter and refine these into meaningful strategies.

- **Maintaining Originality**: Relying solely on AI can lead to repetitive or derivative outputs. Human intuition injects originality and fresh perspectives.

- **Ethical Oversight**: Humans ensure that automated processes adhere to ethical guidelines and avoid unintended harm.

Example: A company might use AI to draft initial business strategies but rely on human teams to ensure these align with their mission and values.

4. Creating Synergy Between Automation and Intuition

The true power of AI brainstorming lies in the collaboration between automation and intuition. This synergy maximizes the strengths of both approaches.

- **Guided Automation**: Use intuition to craft specific, context-aware prompts that direct AI outputs toward meaningful solutions.

- **Iterative Collaboration**: Treat AI-generated ideas as a starting point, refining them through human creativity and expertise.

- **Feedback Loops**: Continuously evaluate and improve AI's performance using insights derived from human intuition.

  Example: A team might use AI to brainstorm initial concepts for a marketing campaign and then refine these ideas through collaborative discussions, ensuring they align with brand identity and audience preferences.

5. Practical Strategies for Balancing Automation and Intuition

1. **Define Clear Roles**: Determine which aspects of brainstorming are best handled by AI and which require human oversight.

2. **Set Boundaries**: Limit AI's role to supportive tasks, such as idea generation, while humans handle decision-making and ethical considerations.

3. **Cultivate Intuition**: Encourage team members to rely on their expertise and instincts, even when working with AI.

4. **Leverage Strengths**: Use AI for efficiency and diversity, while relying on intuition for creativity and judgment.

5. **Iterate Together**: Combine AI outputs with human insights in an iterative process to create well-rounded solutions.

    Balancing automation and intuition is not about choosing one over the other; it's about creating a partnership. By recognizing the unique contributions of both AI and human intuition, teams can unlock a new level of creativity and problem-solving potential, ensuring that technology enhances rather than diminishes the human element in brainstorming.

Cultivating Originality in AI-Assisted Processes

Originality lies at the heart of creativity, distinguishing innovative ideas from generic solutions. While AI offers powerful tools for brainstorming, its outputs often reflect patterns derived from existing data, which can limit their novelty. This section explores how to nurture originality in AI-assisted processes by combining human ingenuity with AI's capabilities, ensuring unique and impactful results.

1. Recognizing the Limitations of AI in Originality

AI excels at generating ideas by analyzing vast amounts of information, but its outputs are fundamentally influenced by its training data.

*   **Pattern-Based Thinking**: AI operates by identifying and replicating patterns, which can result in derivative or predictable ideas.

- **Context Blindness**: AI lacks the emotional and cultural awareness to fully understand the originality of an idea.

- **Risk of Repetition**: Without careful prompting, AI may generate ideas that feel repetitive or lack innovation.

  Example: An AI tool might suggest marketing slogans that sound professional but fail to capture the unique personality of a brand.

2. The Role of Human Creativity in Originality

Humans bring emotional depth, intuition, and the ability to challenge conventions, which are essential for fostering originality.

- **Reframing Problems**: Humans can approach challenges from unexpected angles, redefining the scope of brainstorming sessions.

- **Adding Personal Perspective**: By infusing personal or team-specific experiences, humans ensure ideas are distinctive and contextually relevant.

- **Evaluating Impact**: Originality isn't just about being different—it's about resonating with the audience. Humans assess whether ideas truly connect.

  Example: A designer might take an AI-generated concept and adapt it based on their understanding of emerging trends or cultural nuances.

3. Enhancing Originality Through Effective Prompting

Crafting prompts with originality in mind can push AI beyond its default outputs, leading to more creative and unconventional results.

- **Encourage Divergent Thinking**: Use prompts that challenge AI to generate ideas outside traditional frameworks.

o *Prompt Example*: "Generate a product concept that combines two unrelated industries, like fitness and virtual reality."

- **Incorporate Constraints**: Limit the scope of the output to encourage more focused and innovative ideas.

o *Prompt Example*: "Propose a solution for sustainable packaging using only biodegradable materials found in marine environments."

- **Iterate and Experiment**: Experiment with different phrasings or parameters to refine AI's responses.

4. Integrating Human Insights to Refine AI Outputs

AI-generated ideas often serve as a foundation for human refinement. Teams can build on these outputs to ensure originality.

- **Challenge AI Outputs**: Evaluate AI-generated ideas critically, asking questions like: "What's missing?" or "How can this be reimagined?"

- **Add Emotional Resonance**: Use human insights to align ideas with the emotional and cultural expectations of the target audience.

- **Combine and Remix**: Merge multiple AI-generated ideas or combine them with human concepts to create something entirely new.

  Example: A team might take three AI-generated campaign ideas and combine elements from each to create a unique and compelling strategy.

5. Fostering a Culture of Originality in AI-Assisted Workflows

Originality thrives in environments that encourage creativity, experimentation, and critical thinking.

- **Promote Curiosity**: Encourage team members to explore unconventional ideas and challenge the status quo.

- **Embrace Failure**: View less successful AI outputs as opportunities for learning and iteration.

- **Encourage Collaboration**: Facilitate brainstorming sessions where AI and human participants build on each other's ideas.

- **Celebrate Innovation**: Recognize and reward creative contributions, whether they come from AI, humans, or their collaboration.

6. Practical Tips for Cultivating Originality

1. **Start with a Clear Vision**: Define the unique goals or qualities you want the output to achieve.

2. **Iterate Boldly**: Treat AI outputs as drafts to refine, reimagine, or push in new directions.

3. **Diversify Inputs**: Use diverse datasets or prompt AI to draw from multiple disciplines for fresh perspectives.

4. **Blend AI and Human Creativity**: Pair AI-generated suggestions with human brainstorming to develop ideas further.

5. **Revisit and Evolve**: Periodically reassess and adapt AI processes to stay ahead of trends and maintain originality.

   Originality in AI-assisted processes isn't an accident—it's a deliberate outcome of human ingenuity guiding AI's capabilities. By leveraging effective prompts, fostering a creative environment, and treating AI outputs as a foundation rather than a final product, teams can unlock innovative solutions that are both unique and impactful. This partnership between AI and human creativity ensures that brainstorming remains fresh, meaningful, and future-focused.

Developing a Co-Creative Mindset

A co-creative mindset embraces the partnership between human ingenuity and AI's computational power, emphasizing collaboration over delegation. By viewing AI as an active collaborator rather than a passive tool, individuals and teams can maximize creativity, enhance problem-solving, and foster innovative outcomes. This section explores the principles, strategies, and benefits of adopting a co-creative mindset in AI-assisted brainstorming.

1. The Essence of Co-Creation

Co-creation is the synergy between human intuition, creativity, and AI's analytical and generative capabilities.

- **Shared Contribution**: Both human and AI inputs are valued, each offering unique strengths to the creative process.

- **Dynamic Interaction**: The process involves a continuous loop of feedback, refinement, and evolution.

- **Empowerment Through Partnership**: AI empowers humans to explore uncharted territories while humans steer AI toward meaningful goals.

  Example: A marketing team uses AI to generate a broad range of campaign ideas, then collaboratively selects and refines the most promising ones.

2. Principles of a Co-Creative Mindset

To cultivate a mindset that embraces co-creation, consider these guiding principles:

- **Mutual Strengths**: Recognize AI as a tool to amplify human capabilities, not replace them.

- **Iterative Refinement**: View creativity as an ongoing process where both human and AI inputs evolve over time.

- **Critical Engagement**: Actively assess and enhance AI outputs rather than accepting them at face value.

- **Collaborative Curiosity**: Foster an environment where exploration and experimentation are encouraged.

3. Shifting from Control to Collaboration

Moving from a control-based approach to a collaborative one requires a shift in mindset and workflow.

- **From Directing to Partnering**: Instead of commanding AI to produce results, engage in a dialogue by providing feedback and asking follow-up prompts.

- *Prompt Example*: "This idea is a good start, but can you explore it from a different perspective or make it more user-focused?"

- **From Perfection to Progress**: Embrace the imperfections in AI outputs as opportunities for human intervention and improvement.

- **From Single-Use to Iteration**: Treat AI-generated ideas as iterative drafts that can be refined and built upon.

4. Building Collaborative Workflows

Co-creative workflows integrate human and AI contributions seamlessly, ensuring both play an active role in the process.

- **Feedback Loops**: Regularly review and refine AI outputs, using human insights to guide subsequent iterations.

- **Role Definition**: Clearly delineate tasks best suited for AI (e.g., data analysis, idea generation) versus those requiring human expertise (e.g., emotional resonance, strategic alignment).

- **Interactive Brainstorming**: Use AI as a real-time collaborator during brainstorming sessions, encouraging team members to challenge and expand upon its suggestions.

    Example: In a product development session, AI might generate a list of features based on customer data, while the team evaluates feasibility and adds creative flourishes.

5. Cultivating Trust in the Co-Creative Process

Trust is vital for effective co-creation, ensuring humans feel confident in leveraging AI while maintaining control over the outcomes.

- **Transparency**: Understand how AI generates its outputs, including the data and algorithms it relies on.

- **Accountability**: Take ownership of the final outputs, ensuring they align with human values and goals.

- **Experimentation**: Build trust by experimenting with AI in low-stakes scenarios to better understand its potential and limitations.

6. Fostering a Co-Creative Culture

A culture that values co-creation ensures the integration of AI into brainstorming is embraced at all levels.

- **Encourage Open Dialogue**: Promote discussions on how AI can complement human efforts rather than replace them.

- **Provide Training**: Equip teams with the skills to effectively interact with AI tools, including prompt engineering and critical evaluation.

- **Celebrate Collaboration**: Highlight successes where human and AI contributions resulted in innovative outcomes.

   Example: A company might showcase a project where AI-assisted brainstorming led to a breakthrough product, crediting both the technology and the team.

7. Practical Strategies for Developing a Co-Creative Mindset

1. **Start Small**: Experiment with AI on simple tasks before incorporating it into complex projects.

2. **Ask the Right Questions**: Use prompts that encourage AI to explore diverse perspectives and unconventional solutions.

3. **Involve the Team**: Facilitate group sessions where team members interact with AI and share feedback on its outputs.

4. **Reflect and Refine**: Regularly assess the effectiveness of AI in your creative process and adapt your approach accordingly.

5. **Celebrate Co-Creation**: Recognize and reward instances where AI and human collaboration resulted in exceptional outcomes.

A co-creative mindset transforms the way individuals and teams approach brainstorming, blending human originality with AI's computational power. By fostering collaboration, curiosity, and trust, this mindset unlocks the full potential of AI-assisted creativity, ensuring that the process is not only productive but also deeply innovative and rewarding.

Ethical Brainstorming with AI

In an age where artificial intelligence is becoming a cornerstone of creativity and innovation, the ethical considerations surrounding its use are more critical than ever. AI has the potential to revolutionize brainstorming by offering fresh perspectives, accelerating idea generation, and uncovering hidden patterns. However, like any tool, its effectiveness—and fairness—depends on how it is used. Without deliberate ethical oversight, AI can perpetuate biases, overlook diverse perspectives, and inadvertently lead teams astray.

Ethical brainstorming with AI is about balance: harnessing the power of AI while safeguarding against its limitations. While AI excels at processing vast amounts of data and generating ideas, it lacks the contextual understanding and moral reasoning that human judgment provides. This makes ethics not just a supplementary consideration but a fundamental aspect of integrating AI into creative processes.

The risks of neglecting ethics in AI brainstorming are profound. When biases embedded in AI algorithms go unchecked, they can reinforce stereotypes, marginalize voices, and create solutions that serve only a narrow subset of people. For example, a marketing campaign designed with AI assistance might unintentionally exclude certain demographics if the training data lacks diversity. Similarly, in product design, AI-generated ideas might favor functionality over inclusivity, resulting in solutions that fail to address the needs of all users.

Moreover, ethical lapses can erode trust in AI, both within teams and among the broader audience. Teams may grow skeptical of AI's outputs if they repeatedly encounter biased or impractical suggestions. Clients and customers, too, may lose confidence in a brand that fails to address these issues. Ethical integrity, therefore, is not just a moral obligation but a strategic advantage in leveraging AI for innovation.

To navigate these challenges, teams must adopt a proactive approach to ethical brainstorming. This involves fostering a culture of critical evaluation, ensuring diversity in inputs, and maintaining transparency in AI's role within the creative process. When used responsibly, AI can become a powerful ally, helping to democratize creativity by amplifying underrepresented ideas and pushing the boundaries of innovation.

This chapter explores why ethics must be at the heart of AI brainstorming. It sets the stage for understanding the biases inherent in AI systems, the tools available to mitigate them, and the steps teams can take to ensure responsible use. By embracing ethical practices, we can unlock AI's full potential, transforming it from a tool of convenience into a force for equitable and impactful innovation.

Understanding Bias in AI Outputs

Bias in AI is not just a technical oversight; it's a reflection of the world we live in. AI systems learn from data—data that is often shaped by human decisions, cultural norms, and historical inequities. While AI can analyze and generate ideas with unparalleled speed and scale, it inherits the limitations and biases embedded in its training data and algorithms. This section explores the origins of bias in AI, how it manifests in brainstorming outputs, and why addressing it is crucial for ethical and effective creativity.

What Causes AI Bias?

Bias in AI outputs stems from multiple sources, often intertwined:

1. **Biased Training Data**
   AI models are only as good as the data they are trained on. If the training data reflects societal biases—such as underrepresentation of certain groups or historical inequalities—the AI will replicate and amplify those biases. For instance, an AI tool designed to brainstorm hiring strategies might suggest methods that favor majority demographics if the training data lacks diversity.

2. **Algorithmic Design Choices**
   Algorithms are built by humans, and the decisions made during their development can unintentionally introduce bias. Factors such as feature selection, weighting of variables, and optimization criteria can skew results in subtle but significant ways.

3. **Feedback Loops**
   AI systems often learn from their own outputs over time. If initial biases are present, they can be reinforced through repeated use, creating a feedback loop that amplifies those biases.

4. **Context Blindness**

    AI lacks the ability to understand context, nuance, and cultural sensitivities. Without careful prompt design and human oversight, AI outputs can inadvertently perpetuate stereotypes or exclude perspectives.

How Bias Manifests in Brainstorming Outputs

When applied to creative tasks like brainstorming, bias in AI can lead to several challenges:

- **Narrow Perspectives:** AI may generate ideas that align with dominant cultural norms, overlooking alternative viewpoints or innovative approaches.

- **Exclusion of Underrepresented Groups:** Outputs may cater to majority demographics, neglecting the needs and contributions of marginalized communities.

- **Reinforcement of Stereotypes:** AI might produce suggestions that perpetuate harmful stereotypes, such as gendered roles in marketing campaigns or product designs.

- **Overgeneralization:** By drawing on large datasets, AI can oversimplify complex issues, producing ideas that lack depth or fail to address nuanced problems.

Why Addressing Bias Matters

1. **Ethical Responsibility**

   Creative outputs have real-world implications. Biased ideas can marginalize certain groups, perpetuate inequality, or harm reputations. Addressing bias ensures that AI-generated solutions are fair, inclusive, and responsible.

2. **Enhancing Innovation**

   Diverse perspectives are a cornerstone of creativity. By mitigating bias, teams can access a broader range of ideas and uncover solutions that might otherwise be overlooked.

3. **Building Trust**

   Ethical practices foster trust among team members, clients, and customers. Demonstrating a commitment to fairness and inclusivity can enhance brand reputation and strengthen relationships.

4. **Legal and Reputational Risks**

   In some cases, biased outputs can lead to legal challenges or public backlash. Proactively addressing bias reduces these risks and positions the organization as a leader in ethical AI use.

Examples of Bias in Action

- A fashion brand using AI to brainstorm marketing strategies discovered that its campaign ideas consistently featured a narrow range of body types, reflecting biases in the training data.

- An AI-generated job description inadvertently used language that discouraged women from applying, such as emphasizing aggressive or competitive traits over collaboration.

- A product design brainstorming session led by AI produced solutions optimized for right-handed users, excluding left-handed individuals from consideration.

By understanding the root causes and manifestations of bias in AI, teams can take the first step toward addressing these challenges. The next section will explore practical tools and techniques for mitigating bias, empowering teams to harness AI responsibly and inclusively.

Tools for Mitigating Bias

Mitigating bias in AI brainstorming is an essential step toward fostering inclusive, innovative, and ethical creative processes. While biases may originate from training data, algorithms, or context blindness, a combination of proactive strategies and practical tools can help address these issues effectively. This section outlines key tools and techniques that teams can use to identify, analyze, and mitigate bias in AI-generated outputs.

1. Preemptive Bias Detection

To address bias, it's critical to identify it before it influences brainstorming outputs. Several tools and techniques can help evaluate AI systems for fairness and inclusivity:

- **AI Fairness 360 (IBM):** An open-source toolkit that detects and mitigates bias in datasets and machine learning models. It provides metrics to evaluate fairness and offers algorithms to adjust for biases.

- **What-If Tool (Google):** This interactive visualization tool helps users understand how machine learning models behave, enabling them to spot potential biases and test hypothetical scenarios.

- **Ethics Checklists:** Custom checklists tailored to organizational needs can prompt teams to assess biases in datasets and algorithms systematically.

2. Diverse Data Curation

Bias often originates in the data AI models are trained on. Curating diverse, representative datasets is one of the most effective ways to mitigate this issue:

- **Data Augmentation:** Supplement existing datasets with information from underrepresented groups to ensure balanced coverage.

- **Synthetic Data Generation:** Use tools like Gretel.ai to create synthetic datasets that introduce diversity while preserving privacy.

- **Dataset Documentation:** Adopt practices like "data sheets for datasets" to document the origins, limitations, and biases inherent in data.

3. Prompt Engineering Techniques

Crafting thoughtful prompts is key to guiding AI systems toward unbiased outputs. Techniques include:

- **Explicit Context Inclusion:** Incorporate instructions that prioritize diversity and fairness, such as "Generate ideas that are inclusive of different cultural, gender, and age perspectives."

- **Multiple Perspectives Prompts:** Request ideas from various angles, e.g., "What are the potential solutions for X from the perspective of marginalized communities?"

- **Bias Testing Prompts:** Test AI outputs by asking it to identify its own biases, e.g., "Does this idea include any assumptions that could exclude certain groups?"

4. Human Oversight and Collaboration

Human review is essential to counteract AI's lack of contextual understanding:

- **Bias Audits:** Designate team members to evaluate AI outputs for potential bias and make necessary adjustments.

- **Team Diversity:** Include diverse voices in brainstorming sessions to challenge AI outputs and enrich the creative process.

- **Feedback Loops:** Establish mechanisms for continuous improvement, where human input refines AI suggestions over time.

5. Algorithmic Bias Mitigation

Adjusting AI models themselves can reduce the likelihood of biased outputs:

- **Reweighing Algorithms:** Use techniques like reweighting or resampling to ensure fairer treatment of underrepresented groups in the data.

- **Counterfactual Fairness Modeling:** Build models that generate the same outcomes regardless of sensitive attributes like race, gender, or age.

- **Regular Updates:** Continuously update algorithms with new data to prevent outdated biases from persisting.

6. Transparency and Explainability Tools

Understanding how AI reaches its conclusions is vital for spotting and addressing biases:

- **LIME (Local Interpretable Model-agnostic Explanations):** Helps explain the predictions of machine learning models, making it easier to identify and correct biases.

- **SHAP (SHapley Additive exPlanations):** Provides insights into how input features influence AI decisions, highlighting areas where biases might exist.

- **Model Cards:** Create documentation that explains the purpose, design, and limitations of AI systems in clear, accessible terms.

7. Continuous Education and Awareness

Fostering an organization-wide commitment to ethical AI use requires ongoing learning:

- **Workshops and Training:** Equip teams with knowledge about AI ethics, bias, and responsible practices.

- **Case Study Reviews:** Regularly analyze examples of AI bias in the industry to identify lessons and best practices.

- **Ethical Guidelines:** Develop and adhere to organizational policies that prioritize inclusivity and fairness in AI applications.

8. Stress Testing AI Outputs

Before deploying AI-driven ideas, test them rigorously:

- **Scenario Testing:** Evaluate how outputs perform across different demographic groups or use cases.

- **Diverse Focus Groups:** Present AI-generated ideas to diverse teams for feedback and refinement.

- **Reverse Brainstorming:** Ask, "How could this idea unintentionally exclude or harm certain groups?" to uncover hidden biases.

By leveraging these tools and techniques, teams can transform AI brainstorming into an ethical, inclusive, and innovative process. The next step is integrating these practices into workflows to ensure they become a natural part of using AI in creative endeavors.

Encouraging Responsible AI Use

Responsible AI use is the cornerstone of ethical innovation, particularly in creative and workplace settings. While AI offers unprecedented opportunities for brainstorming and problem-solving, its misuse or unchecked application can lead to unintended consequences, including perpetuating biases, reducing human creativity, and fostering dependency on technology. This section explores strategies to promote responsible AI use, ensuring that it remains a tool for empowerment rather than harm.

1. Cultivating a Responsibility-First Mindset

Encouraging responsible AI use begins with fostering a culture that prioritizes ethical considerations:

- **Ethical Awareness Training:** Equip teams with a clear understanding of ethical AI practices, such as avoiding harm, promoting fairness, and respecting privacy.

- **Ethics Ambassadors:** Assign individuals or committees within organizations to champion responsible AI use and ensure adherence to ethical guidelines.

- **Shared Accountability:** Reinforce that responsibility for AI-driven decisions lies with the humans who create, deploy, and use the technology, not with the AI itself.

2. Developing Clear Usage Guidelines

Creating clear policies around AI use ensures consistency and accountability:

- **Guidelines for AI in Brainstorming:** Specify when and how AI can be used in brainstorming sessions, emphasizing that it should complement—not replace—human creativity.

- **Limitations and Boundaries:** Define clear limits for AI applications, particularly in areas involving sensitive topics, such as social or cultural implications.

- **Transparency Requirements:** Ensure that all stakeholders are aware when AI is being used, how it contributes to decisions, and any limitations in its capabilities.

3. Balancing Human and AI Contributions

A collaborative approach between humans and AI helps maintain originality and contextual relevance:

- **Complementary Roles:** Use AI for idea generation, data analysis, or scenario simulation, while leaving judgment, ethical considerations, and decision-making to humans.

- **Critical Review:** Encourage teams to critically evaluate AI-generated ideas, ensuring they align with organizational values and real-world practicality.

- **Periodic Dependency Checks:** Assess the extent to which AI is being relied upon to avoid over-dependence and ensure human input remains central.

4. Promoting Inclusivity and Diversity in AI Use

Responsible AI practices must include efforts to represent and consider diverse perspectives:

- **Inclusive Prompts:** Craft prompts that explicitly request diverse viewpoints or solutions tailored to underrepresented groups.

- **Democratizing Access:** Ensure that access to AI tools and resources is available to individuals across all organizational levels, fostering equity in creativity and problem-solving.

- **Regular Feedback Loops:** Gather input from a wide range of users to refine AI systems and outputs continually.

5. Ensuring Transparency in AI Processes

Transparency builds trust and encourages accountability:

- **AI Output Disclosures:** Clearly identify AI-generated ideas and differentiate them from human contributions.

- **Open Algorithms:** Advocate for algorithms that are explainable and interpretable, allowing users to understand how AI reaches its conclusions.

- **Stakeholder Communication:** Regularly inform stakeholders about AI's role in brainstorming processes, including its benefits, limitations, and potential biases.

6. Prioritizing Privacy and Data Ethics

Respecting privacy and ensuring data integrity are essential components of responsible AI use:

- **Minimizing Data Use:** Limit the amount of personal or sensitive data AI systems require for brainstorming tasks.

- **Anonymization Techniques:** Employ data anonymization to protect individual identities while maintaining useful insights.

- **Compliance with Regulations:** Adhere to relevant laws and standards, such as GDPR, when using AI tools that involve user data.

7. Monitoring and Evaluating AI Impacts

Continuous monitoring ensures that AI remains aligned with ethical principles and organizational goals:

- **Impact Assessments:** Regularly evaluate how AI affects creativity, inclusivity, and decision-making processes.

- **Bias Tracking:** Keep track of recurring patterns in AI outputs to identify and mitigate biases over time.

- **Iteration and Improvement:** Use feedback and insights to refine AI systems and improve their ethical performance.

8. Empowering Users with Knowledge and Autonomy

Education and empowerment are key to encouraging responsible AI use:

- **Skill Development:** Provide training on AI tools, including prompt crafting, bias detection, and ethical considerations.

- **Encouraging Curiosity:** Motivate users to explore AI's capabilities responsibly, experimenting with diverse approaches and applications.

- **User Autonomy:** Equip users with the tools and knowledge to independently assess and refine AI outputs.

9. Recognizing AI as a Tool, Not a Replacement

Framing AI as an assistant rather than a substitute is crucial for maintaining ethical use:

- **Human Oversight:** Reinforce that humans are ultimately responsible for final decisions, regardless of AI's contributions.

- **Value-Driven Creativity:** Encourage teams to prioritize original, value-driven ideas over convenience-driven AI outputs.

- **Ethical Leadership:** Demonstrate responsible AI use from leadership levels to set a standard for the entire organization.

By implementing these strategies, organizations can create an environment where AI is used ethically, responsibly, and innovatively, enhancing brainstorming processes without compromising integrity or inclusivity.

Ethical Guidelines for Workplace AI Innovation

The integration of AI into workplace innovation has redefined how teams brainstorm, solve problems, and drive creativity. However, the power of AI also brings ethical challenges that organizations must address to ensure responsible and equitable use. Establishing ethical guidelines for AI innovation in the workplace fosters a culture of accountability, fairness, and sustainability while maximizing the potential of these advanced tools.

1. Define Core Ethical Principles

Organizations should adopt foundational principles to guide all AI-related activities:

- **Fairness:** Ensure that AI outputs are inclusive and free from biases that may marginalize or disadvantage certain groups.

- **Transparency:** Maintain openness about how AI tools function, their limitations, and their role in decision-making processes.

- **Accountability:** Establish clear responsibility for the design, deployment, and outcomes of AI applications.

- **Privacy Protection:** Safeguard employee and consumer data by adhering to stringent data protection standards.

2. Establish Guidelines for Ethical AI Usage

Develop a formal code of conduct to provide clarity on how AI should be used in workplace settings:

- **Purpose Specification:** Define acceptable uses for AI tools, ensuring alignment with organizational goals and values.

- **Usage Boundaries:** Clearly outline tasks where AI can and cannot be applied, such as sensitive decision-making areas that require human empathy or ethical judgment.

- **Audit Mechanisms:** Create processes for regularly reviewing AI outputs and ensuring compliance with ethical standards.

3. Foster Collaborative Human-AI Roles

AI should be seen as a complement to human expertise, not a replacement:

- **Co-Creation Processes:** Encourage collaboration between human teams and AI tools, leveraging AI for tasks like idea generation while relying on human creativity and judgment for refinement.

- **Decision Oversight:** Require human validation of AI-driven insights to avoid over-reliance on technology.

- **Skill Enhancement:** Train employees to effectively collaborate with AI, improving their ability to use the technology responsibly and creatively.

4. Mitigate Biases in AI Systems

Bias in AI outputs can perpetuate inequities if left unchecked. Mitigation strategies include:

- **Diverse Training Data:** Use datasets that represent a wide range of perspectives, demographics, and contexts.

- **Bias Audits:** Conduct regular assessments to identify and address any biases in AI-generated outputs.

- **Feedback Mechanisms:** Allow users to flag biased outputs, creating an iterative improvement process for AI systems.

5. Prioritize Inclusivity in AI Innovation

Inclusivity ensures that AI benefits everyone in the workplace:

- **Accessible Design:** Ensure that AI tools are user-friendly and available to all employees, regardless of technical proficiency.

- **Representation in Development:** Involve diverse teams in designing and deploying AI tools to minimize blind spots.

- **Cultural Sensitivity:** Tailor AI applications to respect and understand the cultural nuances of global teams.

6. Implement Ethical Oversight and Governance

Ethical AI use requires structured oversight to ensure adherence to standards:

- **AI Ethics Committees:** Establish cross-disciplinary teams to oversee AI implementation and address ethical dilemmas.

- **Continuous Monitoring:** Regularly review AI's impact on workplace innovation to identify areas of concern or improvement.

- **Regulatory Compliance:** Stay updated with evolving laws and industry standards governing AI use.

7. Promote Transparency and Education

Open communication and knowledge-sharing are key to ethical AI practices:

- **Explainable AI:** Use AI tools that provide clear explanations for their outputs to build user trust.

- **Employee Training:** Educate teams on ethical AI practices, emphasizing their role in maintaining accountability.

- **Stakeholder Engagement:** Involve employees, customers, and partners in discussions about AI innovation, gathering diverse perspectives.

8. Balance Innovation with Caution

While AI offers transformative potential, organizations must be cautious about unintended consequences:

- **Risk Assessments:** Evaluate potential risks, such as privacy breaches or over-dependence on AI, before implementing new tools.

- **Gradual Rollouts:** Introduce AI systems incrementally, allowing time for testing and adjustment.

- **Safeguard Mechanisms:** Build fail-safes to prevent misuse or unexpected outcomes, such as automated decisions without human oversight.

9. Encourage Ethical Creativity

Ethical AI innovation involves using the technology in ways that align with organizational values:

- **Values-Driven Brainstorming:** Frame AI prompts to emphasize solutions that align with ethical and sustainability goals.

- **Avoiding Manipulative Practices:** Prohibit using AI to exploit consumers or manipulate employees.

- **Positive Impact Goals:** Focus on using AI for socially beneficial innovation, such as accessibility or environmental sustainability initiatives.

10. Commit to Continuous Learning and Improvement

Ethical AI practices must evolve with technology and societal expectations:

- **Periodic Evaluations:** Regularly update guidelines to reflect new developments in AI capabilities and ethical considerations.

- **Learning from Failures:** Use past missteps as learning opportunities to refine policies and practices.

- **Global Benchmarking:** Stay informed about ethical AI practices worldwide to adopt best-in-class approaches.

By adopting these ethical guidelines, organizations can harness the transformative power of AI in a way that enhances creativity and innovation while safeguarding fairness, accountability, and trust.

Empowering Ethical Innovators

Ethical innovation is not solely about establishing guidelines and frameworks; it is about cultivating a mindset where individuals feel empowered to navigate the complex interplay of technology and ethics. Empowering ethical innovators involves equipping individuals and teams with the skills, resources, and autonomy to apply AI responsibly while fostering creativity and growth.

1. Cultivating Ethical Awareness

The foundation of empowerment lies in understanding the ethical dimensions of AI innovation:

- **Workshops and Training:** Regular sessions on ethical AI practices help employees recognize potential biases, unintended consequences, and moral dilemmas.

- **Scenario-Based Learning:** Use real-world examples to explore ethical challenges, encouraging teams to think critically about their decisions.

- **Ethical Literacy Programs:** Provide resources on AI ethics, such as reading materials, case studies, and access to expert talks.

2. Promoting a Culture of Responsibility

Ethical innovation thrives in an environment where accountability is encouraged and celebrated:

- **Ownership of Decisions:** Empower teams to take responsibility for AI-driven outputs, ensuring they evaluate and validate outcomes.

- **Encouraging Dialogue:** Create safe spaces for employees to discuss ethical concerns without fear of retaliation, fostering a culture of openness.

- **Celebrating Ethical Wins:** Recognize and reward individuals and teams who champion responsible AI use and make ethically sound decisions.

3. Encouraging Creativity Within Ethical Boundaries

Innovation often involves pushing boundaries, but ethical constraints can spark even greater creativity:

- **Values-Driven Challenges:** Frame brainstorming sessions around ethical goals, such as sustainability or inclusivity, to inspire purposeful innovation.

- **Creative Constraints:** Use ethical considerations as a creative challenge, encouraging teams to find solutions that balance innovation with responsibility.

- **Ethics as Inspiration:** Showcase examples of how ethical AI practices have led to groundbreaking ideas, inspiring others to do the same.

4. Providing Tools for Ethical Decision-Making

Practical tools and frameworks empower innovators to make informed ethical choices:

- **Ethical Decision Trees:** Develop step-by-step guides for evaluating the potential impacts of AI applications.

- **Bias Checklists:** Equip teams with easy-to-use lists to identify and address biases in data, models, and outputs.

- **AI Audit Tools:** Leverage technology to assess the fairness, transparency, and accountability of AI systems.

5. Fostering Leadership in Ethical Innovation

Leaders play a critical role in modeling and driving ethical practices:

- **Ethical Leadership Training:** Provide leaders with the skills to guide teams in navigating ethical dilemmas.

- **Visible Commitment:** Encourage leaders to publicly advocate for and embody ethical AI practices, setting the tone for the organization.

- **Mentorship Programs:** Pair emerging innovators with experienced mentors to foster a culture of responsible and creative AI use.

6. Encouraging Experimentation with Guardrails

Empower individuals to experiment with AI while maintaining ethical oversight:

- **Safe Innovation Sandboxes:** Create controlled environments where teams can test ideas without risking unintended consequences.

- **Iterative Feedback Loops:** Encourage continuous testing, learning, and refining of AI-driven projects to align with ethical standards.

- **Failure as a Learning Tool:** Normalize ethical missteps as opportunities for growth and improvement rather than grounds for punishment.

7. Democratizing Access to Ethical AI

Empowerment requires equitable access to the tools and knowledge needed for ethical AI innovation:

- **Accessible Training:** Ensure that ethical AI resources are available to all employees, regardless of their technical background.

- **Diverse Perspectives:** Actively involve underrepresented groups in AI innovation to ensure inclusivity and reduce blind spots.

- **Community Building:** Encourage collaboration across teams and industries to share insights and best practices for ethical AI use.

8. Embedding Ethics into Organizational DNA

Ethical innovation should be an intrinsic part of how organizations operate:

- **Ethics-First Mission Statements:** Align organizational goals with ethical principles to signal a commitment to responsible innovation.

- **Integrated Ethical Practices:** Make ethical considerations a standard part of project planning, execution, and evaluation.

- **Employee Empowerment Policies:** Develop policies that explicitly support employees in raising ethical concerns and innovating responsibly.

9. Inspiring Long-Term Commitment to Ethics

Sustainable ethical innovation requires a commitment to ongoing learning and improvement:

- **Continuous Education:** Provide ongoing training to keep teams updated on the evolving ethical landscape of AI.

- **Long-Term Vision:** Encourage teams to consider the future impact of their innovations, ensuring they align with societal and environmental well-being.

- **Ethical Legacy Projects:** Highlight initiatives that have successfully integrated ethical practices, inspiring future innovators.

By fostering a culture that values responsibility, creativity, and inclusion, organizations can empower ethical innovators to not only excel in their roles but also contribute meaningfully to a future where AI drives progress without compromising ethical integrity.

The Future of Creativity with AI

As we come to the end of this exploration into the transformative power of AI in creativity and problem-solving, it's worth taking a moment to reflect on the journey we've taken together. This book began by identifying a fundamental challenge in modern workplaces: the limitations of traditional brainstorming and ideation methods in addressing the complex, fast-paced demands of today's world. These methods, while foundational, often fail to keep up with the need for speed, precision, and innovation that modern industries require.

In response to this bottleneck, we examined how artificial intelligence (AI) is changing the game. AI is no longer a futuristic concept or a tool confined to the realm of data scientists and technologists. It has evolved into a practical, accessible resource for professionals across industries, enabling them to think beyond conventional boundaries and uncover insights that were previously out of reach. By combining the raw computational power of AI with human ingenuity, we unlock opportunities for creative exploration that redefine what is possible.

Central to this transformation is the art of **prompt engineering**. As we've seen, crafting the right questions or commands allows us to harness AI's potential in meaningful ways. Whether it's refining vague ideas into actionable concepts, generating unique ad campaigns, or designing intricate solutions to real-world challenges, prompt engineering provides a bridge between human creativity and AI's vast capabilities. The examples and strategies shared throughout this book have demonstrated how the right prompts can turn AI into a collaborator, a brainstorming partner, and even an innovation catalyst.

We also explored specific applications of AI in various creative and professional contexts. From marketing ideation to stakeholder management and beyond, AI has proven its versatility in tackling a wide array of challenges. Along the way, we addressed not only the benefits but also the ethical considerations and limitations of relying on AI in creative industries. By acknowledging these nuances, we've painted a realistic picture of how to incorporate AI thoughtfully and responsibly into professional workflows.

Now, as we look ahead, we must recognize that this journey is far from over. AI continues to evolve at a rapid pace, bringing new possibilities and challenges with every advancement. For individuals and organizations willing to embrace this change, the opportunities are immense. This book serves as a starting point—a guide to understanding and applying AI in creativity and problem-solving. But the true power of AI lies in what comes next: how you, the reader, will take these insights and use them to innovate, inspire, and shape the future.

In reflecting on this journey, one thing becomes clear: AI is not here to replace us. It is here to enhance us. It empowers us to think bigger, work smarter, and achieve more than we ever could on our own. By embracing AI as a co-creator and integrating it into our processes with curiosity and intentionality, we step into a future where creativity knows no bounds. The next chapters of this story are yours to write, armed with the knowledge and tools to redefine what's possible in your personal and professional life.

The Evolving Role of AI in Workplaces

AI's integration into the workplace is not a hypothetical future—it's already reshaping how we work, collaborate, and innovate. What started as a means of automating routine tasks has evolved into a sophisticated tool that augments human capabilities, redefines roles, and creates new opportunities for growth. This transformation is not just about efficiency but about enabling a more dynamic, creative, and adaptive workforce. In this section, we'll explore how AI is evolving in workplaces, what it means for professionals across industries, and how it can serve as a partner in shaping the future of work.

AI as a Co-Creator, Not a Replacement

One of the most profound shifts AI brings to the workplace is its role as a collaborator. Unlike earlier fears of AI replacing jobs, it has become clear that its true value lies in complementing human creativity and decision-making.

- **Enhancing Creativity and Problem-Solving**: AI tools like generative AI can produce ideas, designs, and solutions at a scale and speed unattainable by humans alone. For example, marketing teams use AI to generate ad concepts, while engineers employ it to design complex systems. Yet, the human touch remains crucial for curating, refining, and implementing these ideas.

- **Supporting Decision-Making**: AI-powered analytics tools provide actionable insights by processing massive datasets and identifying trends. This allows professionals to make more informed decisions without being overwhelmed by information.

- **Routine Task Automation**: AI excels at handling repetitive tasks such as data entry, scheduling, or generating reports. By automating these responsibilities, it frees up human workers to focus on high-impact, strategic activities.

Rather than rendering human roles obsolete, AI enables people to shift their attention toward areas that require empathy, creativity, and nuanced thinking—qualities that remain uniquely human.

Democratizing Access to Innovation

AI is also leveling the playing field by democratizing access to powerful tools that were once available only to large organizations with significant resources.

- **Affordable Solutions for Small Businesses**: Cloud-based AI platforms have made it possible for startups and small businesses to leverage sophisticated tools for marketing, customer service, and product development.

- **Equalizing Opportunities Across Industries**: From healthcare to education, AI is enabling smaller players to innovate and compete with larger entities. For instance, a small architecture firm can use AI-driven design tools to create advanced models previously reserved for big-budget projects.

- **Empowering Individuals**: Freelancers, creatives, and independent professionals are increasingly adopting AI tools to enhance their workflows, from designing graphics to drafting business proposals. This empowerment allows individuals to operate at a scale once reserved for teams.

By democratizing innovation, AI ensures that creativity and growth are not limited by budget or scale.

Future Skills for a Changing Workforce

As AI takes on a greater role in workplaces, the skills required to thrive in professional environments are evolving. The future workforce must adapt to this change by developing new competencies.

- **Technical Proficiency**: While not everyone needs to become a data scientist, understanding how to use AI tools effectively—such as prompt engineering, interpreting AI-driven insights, or managing AI workflows—will be essential.

- **Collaboration with AI**: Workers will need to view AI as a teammate rather than a tool. This means understanding its strengths and limitations, knowing when to rely on AI, and how to guide its outputs.

- **Critical Thinking and Ethical Judgement**: As AI becomes more integrated into decision-making, humans must ensure that its use aligns with ethical standards, organizational values, and societal norms.

- **Emotional Intelligence and Creativity**: While AI can generate ideas and solutions, the ability to connect emotionally with others, inspire teams, and think outside the box remains firmly in the human domain.

These emerging skills will redefine what it means to be a professional in an AI-driven workplace, emphasizing the synergy between human intelligence and machine capabilities.

Navigating the Challenges of AI Integration

Despite its potential, integrating AI into workplaces is not without challenges. Understanding these hurdles is crucial for leveraging AI effectively and responsibly.

- **Workplace Resistance**: Employees may fear that AI will replace their jobs or disrupt established workflows. Clear communication, training programs, and transparency about AI's role can alleviate these concerns.

- **Skill Gaps**: Organizations must invest in reskilling and upskilling their workforce to ensure employees can fully utilize AI tools.

- **Bias and Ethical Concerns**: AI systems are only as unbiased as the data they are trained on. Companies must ensure that their AI systems promote fairness and inclusivity.

- **Data Privacy and Security**: With AI relying heavily on data, organizations must prioritize robust security measures and compliance with privacy regulations to maintain trust.

Addressing these challenges head-on will pave the way for a smoother and more effective integration of AI into workplaces.

A Collaborative Future: Humans and AI Together

The evolving role of AI in workplaces highlights a broader truth: the future of work is not an either-or scenario between humans and machines but a collaborative partnership.

- **Amplifying Human Potential**: By taking over routine and data-intensive tasks, AI allows humans to focus on strategic, creative, and empathetic work.

- **Fostering Innovation**: AI's ability to analyze vast amounts of data and generate ideas sparks innovation that might otherwise be overlooked.

- **Creating New Opportunities**: Entirely new roles, industries, and business models are emerging as a result of AI, from AI trainers and ethics officers to AI-driven creative agencies.

As AI continues to evolve, workplaces will become more dynamic, adaptable, and innovative. Those who embrace AI as a co-creator rather than a competitor will unlock its full potential, driving success in ways that were once unimaginable.

By recognizing and preparing for AI's evolving role, organizations and individuals can thrive in this new era of work, ensuring that technology serves as a tool for growth and creativity rather than a source of fear or disruption. This balance of human ingenuity and machine power is the foundation of the future workplace.

AI's Transformative Impact on Creative Industries

The creative industries—encompassing advertising, design, media, entertainment, publishing, and more—have long been driven by human ingenuity and artistic expression. Yet, as artificial intelligence continues to evolve, it is reshaping how these industries operate, innovate, and produce. From democratizing access to creative tools to opening up entirely new forms of artistic expression, AI is fundamentally altering the landscape of creativity. This chapter will explore how AI is transforming creative industries, the opportunities it presents, and the challenges it brings.

Revolutionizing Traditional Fields of Creativity

AI has redefined the boundaries of what is possible within traditional creative fields, offering tools that streamline workflows and enhance output quality.

- **Advertising and Marketing**: AI-powered platforms like ChatGPT and MidJourney are generating ad copy, visual concepts, and personalized marketing strategies at unprecedented speed. Brands can now develop entire campaigns tailored to specific audiences within hours, leveraging AI's ability to analyze data and predict trends.

- **Media and Publishing**: Automated content creation tools are being used to draft articles, generate headlines, and even write full-length novels. AI is also assisting with editing and proofreading, ensuring faster turnaround times for publications.

- **Design and Architecture**: In design, AI-driven software generates mockups, prototypes, and 3D models, enabling creators to experiment with countless variations in a fraction of the time. Similarly, architects are using AI to design sustainable and efficient structures by simulating real-world scenarios.

- **Film and Animation**: AI has transformed visual effects and animation by automating labor-intensive processes like rotoscoping, rendering, and motion capture. Filmmakers are also using AI to analyze scripts, predict audience reception, and even compose scores.

In each of these fields, AI is not replacing creators but providing them with new tools to execute their vision more efficiently and effectively.

New Frontiers of Creativity Enabled by AI

Beyond enhancing existing processes, AI is opening up entirely new creative possibilities that were previously unimaginable.

- **Generative Art**: AI algorithms are being used to create original pieces of art, from abstract paintings to hyper-realistic portraits. These works challenge traditional notions of authorship and creativity, sparking debates about the role of machines in art.

- **Interactive Storytelling**: AI is enabling creators to craft personalized, immersive narratives in video games, virtual reality experiences, and even live performances. For example, AI-driven characters can respond dynamically to player actions, creating unique experiences for each individual.

- **Real-Time Customization**: AI allows content to be tailored in real time based on audience preferences. For example, streaming platforms are experimenting with adaptive storytelling, where viewers influence the plot of a show as they watch.

- **Collaborative Creations**: AI-powered platforms like OpenAI's MuseNet are enabling musicians to co-create compositions, blending human input with machine-generated melodies to produce unique soundscapes.

These new frontiers demonstrate that AI is not merely a tool for productivity but a collaborator that expands the boundaries of what creativity can achieve.

Ethical and Cultural Considerations

The integration of AI into creative industries brings with it significant ethical and cultural challenges that must be addressed to ensure responsible use.

- **Bias and Representation**: AI models trained on biased data can inadvertently reinforce stereotypes or marginalize certain voices. Creators must actively ensure that their tools promote inclusivity and diversity.

- **Cultural Authenticity**: As AI generates content across languages and cultures, there is a risk of diluting cultural authenticity. For example, an AI-generated film set in a specific culture may lack the nuance and depth that human creators bring.

- **Ownership and Copyright**: Questions about authorship and intellectual property rights are increasingly complex in the age of AI-generated art and content. Who owns an artwork created by an AI, and how should it be credited?

- **Job Displacement**: While AI creates opportunities, it also disrupts traditional roles within creative industries. Professionals must adapt to these changes by learning to work alongside AI rather than viewing it as a threat.

By addressing these concerns, the creative industries can harness AI's potential while preserving ethical integrity and cultural richness.

The Rise of Hybrid Creative Teams

AI's transformative impact on creative industries is leading to the rise of hybrid teams where humans and machines collaborate seamlessly.

- **Creative Efficiency**: AI takes on repetitive tasks such as brainstorming ideas, analyzing audience data, or generating initial drafts, freeing humans to focus on refinement and strategy.

- **Enhanced Collaboration**: AI-powered tools enable teams to collaborate across time zones and disciplines, providing a unified platform for ideation and execution.

- **Data-Driven Creativity**: By analyzing consumer behavior and market trends, AI helps teams create content that resonates with their target audiences, ensuring relevance and impact.

These hybrid teams exemplify the synergy between human intuition and machine precision, setting a new standard for creative excellence.

A Paradigm Shift in Creative Industries

The ongoing evolution of AI in creative industries signals a paradigm shift where technology becomes an integral part of the creative process.

- **From Craft to Curation**: Creators are transitioning from crafting content manually to curating and refining AI-generated ideas. This shift requires a new skill set focused on critical thinking, judgment, and aesthetic sensibility.

- **Scaling Creativity**: AI allows creators to scale their output without compromising quality, enabling them to reach larger audiences and explore diverse projects.

- **Continuous Learning**: As AI tools evolve, creative professionals must engage in lifelong learning to stay ahead of trends and maximize the potential of emerging technologies.

This paradigm shift emphasizes the need for a mindset that embraces change, curiosity, and adaptability.

The Future of Creativity with AI

AI's impact on creative industries is only just beginning. As technology advances, the boundaries between human and machine creativity will continue to blur, giving rise to unprecedented possibilities. The future belongs to those who can balance the efficiency and innovation of AI with the emotional depth and authenticity of human creativity. By doing so, we can create a world where art, culture, and innovation thrive in harmony with technology.

AI is not the end of creativity—it is the beginning of a new chapter, where the collaboration between humans and machines redefines what it means to create.

Embracing AI as a Partner in Innovation

Innovation has always been at the heart of human progress. From the earliest tools to the rise of the internet, every transformative leap has relied on human ingenuity. Now, artificial intelligence (AI) has emerged not just as a tool for productivity but as a powerful partner in the process of innovation itself. Embracing AI as a collaborator rather than merely a resource requires a shift in mindset, strategy, and approach. This chapter explores how individuals and organizations can adopt AI as a partner in driving innovation, leveraging its capabilities to unlock creativity, solve complex problems, and reimagine the future.

AI as a Creative Catalyst

AI's role in innovation lies in its ability to amplify human creativity and enable breakthroughs that were previously unattainable.

- **Idea Generation**: AI excels at generating a high volume of ideas in response to prompts, from product concepts to business strategies. By offering fresh perspectives, it challenges traditional thinking and sparks novel solutions.

- **Exploration Without Constraints**: Human creativity is often limited by biases, assumptions, or lack of resources. AI, on the other hand, can explore countless possibilities without preconceived notions, uncovering paths that may have been overlooked.

- **Creative Augmentation**: Tools like generative AI allow creators to produce prototypes, visual designs, or narratives rapidly. For example, designers can use AI to develop multiple iterations of a concept, accelerating the refinement process.

- **Cross-Disciplinary Insights**: AI's ability to synthesize information across fields enables interdisciplinary innovation. A healthcare researcher might use AI to identify patterns in patient data that could inform developments in wearable tech, or an architect might leverage AI insights to integrate sustainable design practices into urban planning.

Rather than replacing human creativity, AI serves as a catalyst, expanding the scope of what's possible and empowering individuals to think bigger.

Shifting from Tool to Teammate

To fully embrace AI as a partner in innovation, we must move beyond treating it as a passive tool and begin working alongside it as an active teammate.

- **Understanding AI's Strengths**: AI thrives in analyzing large datasets, identifying patterns, and executing repetitive tasks with precision. Acknowledging these strengths allows humans to delegate appropriately, focusing on areas where emotional intelligence, critical thinking, and ethical judgment are essential.

- **Collaborative Workflows**: Incorporating AI into innovation processes requires new workflows where human and machine contributions complement one another. For example, a marketing team might use AI to generate dozens of campaign ideas but rely on human expertise to select the ones that align with brand values.

- **Iterative Development**: AI's capacity for rapid iteration enables teams to experiment and refine ideas quickly. This fosters a culture of trial and error, where failure is seen as an opportunity for learning rather than a setback.

- **Promoting Adaptability**: Just as humans learn to work with AI, AI systems are continually improving through feedback. By viewing AI as a dynamic collaborator, organizations can create an environment where both humans and machines evolve together.

This shift in perception—from seeing AI as merely a tool to embracing it as a teammate—lays the foundation for deeper collaboration and greater innovation.

Fostering an AI-Driven Innovation Culture

Integrating AI into innovation efforts requires more than just technology; it demands a cultural shift within organizations and teams.

- **Encouraging Experimentation**: Leaders must create a culture where employees feel empowered to experiment with AI, even if outcomes are uncertain. Providing access to AI tools and encouraging exploration fosters creativity and resilience.

- **Training and Education**: Equipping teams with the knowledge and skills to use AI effectively is critical. This includes not just technical training but also guidance on how to frame prompts, interpret AI outputs, and integrate insights into workflows.

- **Collaboration Across Teams**: AI-driven innovation thrives in collaborative environments where diverse perspectives come together. Cross-functional teams that combine technical expertise, domain knowledge, and creative thinking are best positioned to leverage AI's potential.

- **Ethical Stewardship**: A culture of innovation must also include a commitment to ethical practices. Teams should actively consider the implications of AI-driven solutions, ensuring they align with organizational values and societal norms.

By embedding these principles into their operations, organizations can create an ecosystem where AI and human creativity coexist harmoniously.

Overcoming Barriers to AI Collaboration

While the potential of AI as a partner in innovation is immense, there are barriers that must be addressed to unlock its full potential.

- **Fear of Job Displacement**: Employees may resist AI adoption due to concerns about losing their roles. Transparent communication about AI's role as a complement to human work, rather than a replacement, is essential to overcoming this fear.

- **Skill Gaps**: Not all employees are familiar with AI tools or how to use them effectively. Investment in training programs and accessible resources can bridge this gap and ensure teams feel confident working with AI.

- **Data Challenges**: The quality of AI outputs depends on the quality of data it's trained on. Organizations must prioritize data accuracy, relevance, and diversity to avoid biased or subpar results.

- **Misalignment of Expectations**: Unrealistic expectations about AI's capabilities can lead to disappointment or misuse. Educating teams about what AI can and cannot do ensures its application is grounded in reality.

By addressing these challenges, organizations can create an environment where AI is not just accepted but embraced as a valuable partner in innovation.

Unlocking the Future of Innovation

The relationship between AI and innovation is still in its early stages, but the potential is already clear: AI is not just a tool for incremental improvements but a driver of transformative change.

- **Pushing Boundaries**: AI enables individuals and organizations to tackle problems that were once deemed unsolvable, from developing sustainable energy solutions to creating personalized education systems.

- **Fostering Inclusion**: By democratizing access to advanced tools, AI ensures that innovation is not limited to large corporations or elite institutions. Anyone with curiosity and creativity can leverage AI to bring their ideas to life.

- **Shaping New Paradigms**: As AI continues to evolve, it will redefine traditional approaches to creativity, problem-solving, and collaboration, ushering in an era of unprecedented possibilities.

Embracing AI as a partner in innovation is not just about adopting new technology—it's about rethinking how we approach challenges, create solutions, and envision the future. Those who can harness the synergy between human creativity and machine intelligence will lead the way in shaping a world that is smarter, more inclusive, and more innovative than ever before.

The Future of Creativity: A Vision Beyond Limits

Creativity is often seen as one of the defining traits of humanity—a force that has driven innovation, art, and progress throughout history. Yet as artificial intelligence continues to evolve, it challenges our understanding of creativity and its boundaries. The future of creativity is no longer confined to human imagination alone; it is being expanded by the limitless potential of AI. This final chapter explores the profound ways in which AI will shape creativity in the years to come, offering a vision of collaboration, innovation, and a redefinition of what it means to create.

Blurring the Lines Between Human and Machine Creativity

As AI systems grow increasingly sophisticated, the distinction between human and machine creativity will become harder to define.

- **Shared Authorship**: The future will see more projects where humans and AI are co-authors, co-designers, and co-creators. From generative art to collaborative writing, these partnerships will produce works that neither could achieve alone.

- **Dynamic Interactions**: AI will evolve from a reactive tool to a proactive collaborator, capable of anticipating needs, suggesting ideas, and iterating based on human feedback in real time. Imagine AI tools that not only assist with a project but also inspire entirely new creative directions.

- **Hybrid Aesthetics**: The blending of human intuition and AI's algorithmic precision will create new artistic styles, narratives, and cultural expressions that transcend traditional boundaries.

Rather than diminishing human creativity, this collaboration enhances it, offering a glimpse into a future where the creative process is more dynamic and inclusive than ever before.

AI-Driven Creativity Across Industries

The impact of AI on creativity will not be confined to traditional artistic fields; it will extend to industries where innovation and problem-solving are essential.

- **Healthcare and Biotech**: AI is already being used to design drugs and develop medical solutions. In the future, it may also contribute to creating patient-centric healthcare experiences through personalized communication and empathetic storytelling.

- **Education**: AI will revolutionize how knowledge is shared and learned, creating tailored learning experiences that adapt to individual needs. Teachers and students will co-create interactive, immersive educational content with AI assistance.

- **Urban Planning and Architecture**: Future cities will be shaped by AI, combining data-driven insights with human creativity to design sustainable, efficient, and aesthetically pleasing environments.

- **Social Innovation**: AI will play a key role in tackling global challenges, from climate change to inequality. Creative applications of AI will drive solutions that are both effective and inclusive, empowering communities to participate in shaping their futures.

This expansion of AI-driven creativity highlights its potential to not only solve problems but to reimagine the way we live, work, and connect with one another.

Empowering the Individual Creator

One of the most transformative aspects of AI is its ability to democratize creativity, empowering individuals to bring their ideas to life regardless of their resources or expertise.

- **Accessible Tools**: AI-powered platforms will become more intuitive and accessible, enabling anyone—from aspiring artists to budding entrepreneurs—to create professional-quality work without the need for specialized training.

- **Personalized Creativity**: AI will adapt to individual preferences, styles, and goals, serving as a personal creative assistant that evolves alongside the user. For instance, an AI tool might learn a writer's unique voice and suggest edits that align with their tone.

- **Global Collaboration**: The future will see the rise of decentralized creative communities, where individuals from different parts of the world collaborate with AI to produce cross-cultural works.

By lowering barriers to entry and fostering inclusivity, AI ensures that creativity is no longer the domain of the privileged few but a universal opportunity.

Challenges in the Creative Future

While the future of AI-driven creativity is full of promise, it also raises critical challenges that must be addressed.

- **Ethics and Authenticity**: As AI-generated content becomes indistinguishable from human work, questions of authenticity and originality will arise. How do we ensure that creativity retains its human essence in an AI-driven world?

- **Intellectual Property**: The legal frameworks surrounding AI-generated works remain underdeveloped. Establishing clear guidelines for ownership and credit will be crucial in fostering trust and fairness.

- **Bias and Representation**: AI systems are only as unbiased as the data they are trained on. Ensuring that AI-driven creativity is inclusive and reflective of diverse perspectives will require intentional effort and oversight.

- **Over-Reliance on AI**: There is a risk that over-reliance on AI could stifle human ingenuity, as creators may become complacent or defer entirely to machine-generated solutions. Balancing the roles of human intuition and machine intelligence will be essential.

Navigating these challenges will require a collaborative effort between technologists, creatives, policymakers, and society at large.

A Call to Action: Embracing AI as a Co-Creator

The future of creativity is not a zero-sum game between humans and AI. Instead, it is an opportunity to redefine what creativity means in a world where technology and imagination intersect.

- **Adopt a Growth Mindset**: Embracing AI as a co-creator requires a willingness to learn, experiment, and adapt. Creatives must approach AI with curiosity rather than fear, seeing it as an ally in their work.

- **Foster Ethical Innovation**: The development and use of AI in creative fields must be guided by ethical principles that prioritize fairness, inclusivity, and transparency.

- **Collaborate Across Disciplines**: The most exciting innovations will emerge at the intersection of fields. By fostering interdisciplinary collaboration, we can unlock the full potential of AI-driven creativity.

- **Celebrate Human-AI Synergy**: Rather than viewing AI as a competitor, we should celebrate the unique strengths that both humans and machines bring to the table. Together, they can achieve far more than either could alone.

This vision of creativity is not bound by limits but fueled by possibilities. By embracing AI as a partner in innovation, we can create a future where creativity knows no bounds—a future where imagination, technology, and humanity come together to build something truly extraordinary.

Discover more

Autor

Other books